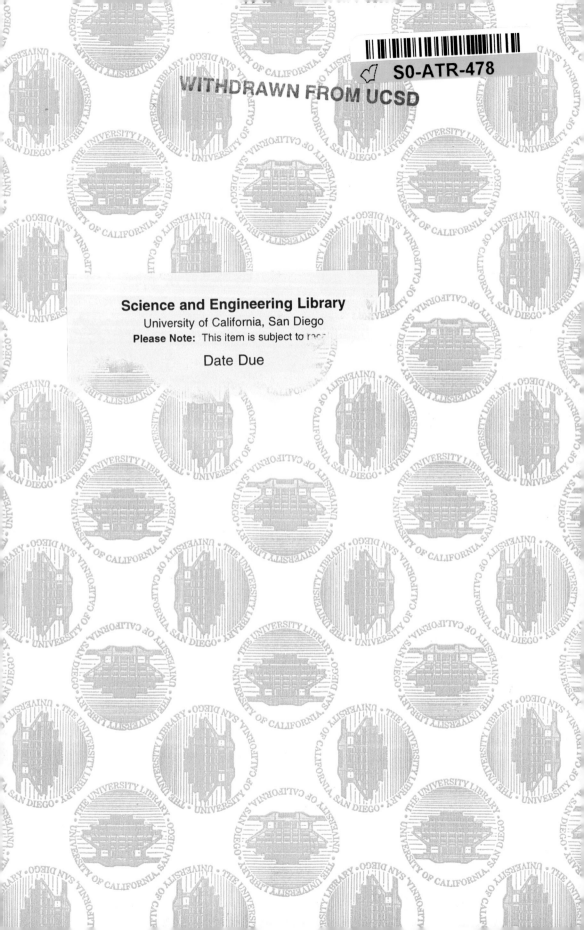

Transactions

of the

American Philosophical Society

Held at Philadelphia

For Promoting Useful Knowledge

Vol. 88, Pt. 1

Babylonian Horoscopes

FRANCESCA ROCHBERG

American Philosophical Society

Independence Square 🙰 Philadelphia

1998

ISBN:0-87169-881-1

Library of Congress Cataloging-in-Publication Data

Rochberg, Francesca, 1952-
    Babylonian horoscopes / Francesca Rochberg.
        p.   cm. -- (Transactions of the American Philosophical
    Society, ISSN 0065-9746 ; v. 88, pt. 1)
    Includes bibliographical references and index.
    ISBN 0-87169-881-1 (pbk.)
    1. Akkadian language--Texts. 2. Astrology, Assyro-Babylonian.
I. Title. II. Series.
PJ3921.A8R63   1998
492'.1--dc21
                                                        97-44943
                                                            CIP

TABLE of CONTENTS

For my dear ones

Jacob, Gemma, and Perce

ACKNOWLEDGMENTS

I owe a tremendous debt of gratitude to David Pingree who gave me Sachs' handwritten notes on the texts identified and studied at the British Museum. These transliterations were the springboard for this text edition and a great aid throughout my work on the horoscopes. I also want to express my appreciation to Prof. Pingree for discussing with me the dating of the documents by means of Bryant Tuckerman's *Planetary, Lunar and Solar Positions: 601 BC to AD 1* (Memoirs of the American Philosophical Society, 56 [1962]), as well as a great many other details. After acquiring Peter Huber's pc programs PLANETS, LUNEC and SOLEC, however, I replaced the use of Tuckerman's tables with Huber's program. I want to thank Prof. Huber for his generosity in making such an invaluable tool available. Thanks are also due Erica Reiner, Hermann Hunger, Bernard R. Goldstein, and Alan C. Bowen for reading manuscript drafts and offering me the benefit of their wisdom and experience. I also thank Hermann Hunger for final collations of all the texts which I had not been able to see for several years since my own collation of the corpus in 1987. As well, and as always, I thank the Trustees of the British Museum for permission to study and publish the tablets from the British Museum. I also want to thank Mme. B. André-Leicknam, conservateur of inscriptions at the Louvre, for providing photographs and persmission to publish AO 17649, and Prof. William Hallo for providing excellent photographs and granting permission to publish the three Yale horoscopes. I also wish to extend special thanks to Hallo for his hospitality to me during my year of study at Yale. I want to express deep appreciation to Asger Aaboe for giving of his time during my sabbatical year as Visiting Fellow in History of Science at Yale in 1989-90. While the edition of the horoscopes was not completed that year at Yale as originally intended, what I learned from Aaboe about Babylonian astronomy became crucial to my work on the horoscope texts. Finally, I want to acknowledge the help I received from J.P. Britton, with whom any discussion of astronomical and textual problems becomes profitable.

I was fortunate in the extreme to receive as a Fellow the support of the MacArthur Foundation during the very early stages of this project. The work was completed during my year as Guggenheim Fellow in 1993-94. I am happy to express my great appreciation to both granting agencies.

All responsibility for errors in readings, dating, and interpretation, of course remains with me.

PREFACE

The extant Babylonian horoscopes are brought together for the first time in this edition so that they may be studied as a class of texts. This is not a synthetic or analytic study of Babylonian "astrology." The primary purpose of this work is to edit and translate the horoscope texts. Abraham Sachs worked on practically all the known horoscopes as part of his lifelong careful attention to all late Babylonian texts of astronomical content. As far as I know, Sachs identified all but three of the documents in the corpus identified since the 1950s, but only those appearing in his 1952 article "Babylonian Horoscopes" (*JCS* 6: pp.49-75, pls.III-IV) were published in transliteration and translation. For the sake of bringing all the horoscope texts together, those published by Sachs are included here, in most cases, with virtually no changes.

The Babylonian horoscopes should be incorporated into any study of the history of Babylonian celestial divination as part of a systematic corpus of cuneiform astrological texts. Their relations are clearly to omens, in particular nativity omens, which foretell personal matters on the basis of the appearance of a planet or a fixed star at the birth of the individual concerned. No other genre of astrological cuneiform text besides the horoscopes presents the complex situation of the heavens on the date and sometimes at the time of a birth. Still, the prognostications for the native, when they are included in the Babylonian horoscope, clearly derive from the nativity omen tradition, and by extension, the tradition of celestial omens (*Enūma Anu Enlil*) in general. But unlike the nativity, or celestial, omens, which do not depend upon the use of computational astronomical methods, the Babylonian horoscopes represent the single genre of astrological cuneiform texts to take account of the positions of all the planets on the date of a birth, and therefore necessitate the derivation, rather than observation of those positions. The nature of this dependence on astronomy is unique among the Babylonian astrological texts, and further argues for the uniqueness of the horoscope genre.

A skeletal framework for a history of Babylonian scholarly celestial divination would begin with late Old Babylonian omen texts (ca. 1800 B.C.), and continues through the Middle Babylonian and Middle Assyrian periods (ca. 1200 B.C.) with forerunners to the canonical celestial omen series *Enūma Anu Enlil*. Isolated references to celestial "signs" in Sumerian sources, such as the sign sent in the form of a bright star to Gudea for the building of Ningirsu's temple (Gudea *Cyl*. A v 23- vi 2; ix 9-10), do not constitute sufficient evidence to warrant speaking of the origins of celestial divination in a Sumerian milieu. Only with the development of Babylonian scribal scholarship does evidence for the systematic consideration of celestial phenomena as omens appear in tablets of the late Old Babylonian period.

The interest in celestial phenomena as a means of determining what the gods held in store for the king and the entire kingdom gave rise to the compilation of such omens in a reference work, which ultimately took shape as a collection of some seven thousand celestial omens in a series of seventy tablets known as *Enūma Anu Enlil*. This product of Old and Middle Babylonian scribal scholarship was designed for use by scholars who observed or computed celestial phenomena for the purpose of prognostication. By the middle of the second millennium, celestial divination had become a major feature of the learned culture of Mesopotamia. Soon the tradition extended beyond the Babylonian scribal centers to those of the bordering states of Hatti and Elam, as evidenced in texts from sites in Anatolia and Iran of the Middle Assyrian and Middle Babylonian periods.

In the seventh century B.C., an abundance of texts reveals the activities of the Sargonid court astrologers as well as their use of the fully developed form of the *Enūma Anu Enlil* series placed in the palace library of Assurbanipal. What might be referred to as the late period of Babylonian celestial divination ranges over a number of historical periods as well as of textual genres. Late Babylonian astrological texts include a wide variety of celestial as well as nativity omens and horoscopes. These genres span the Achaemenid, Seleucid, and Arsacid periods (ca. 500 B.C. to 50 B.C.). The focus in these genres upon mundane prognostication, whether for the king, the state, or the individual, in the case of nativity omens and horoscopes, differentiates them from texts of astronomical content alone. This distinction between textual genres was made by the scribes themselves, who rarely combined on a single tablet purely astronomical procedures with omens. This is not to say that the texts which made prognostications, the "astrological" texts, constituted a separate science. Celestial divination, astronomical observation, and astronomical computation represent interdependent parts of a multifaceted and complex tradition of celestial science in ancient Mesopotamia.

The appearance of horoscopes in Babylonia at the end of the fifth century B.C. marks the point when the situation of the heavens at the time of a birth came to be regarded as significant for the future of an individual. Before this time, little evidence supports the idea that the individual had a place in the scope of traditional celestial divination, though there had been divination which derived predictions for individuals based on date of birth and on physiognomy. A direct connection between the individual and the heavens, however, is not reflected either in physiognomic or in birth omens.

The relationship between personal piety and personal happiness within the divine scheme of the universe is a subject of concern in the Babylonian "wisdom" literature, and although the relationship is viewed with a certain skepticism in some ancient sources, the idea that an individual's life, as all other things, is affected by the gods seems to be a basic assumption. If, as in the celestial omen collection *Enūma Anu Enlil*, celestial phenomena had been taken to indicate the future for the king and the state of affairs in the country at large, it seems *a priori* possible that such a belief could be carried over and applied to the life of an individual. That such an idea was applied to the individual, at that particular time—coincident with the loss of Babylonian control of their own political future to the Achaemenid Persians— underscores the politically charged nature of traditional celestial omens. These had given expression both to a concern for the stability of the Babylonian (or Assyrian) king and his state, and to the belief in a connection between the kingdom and the cosmos. The horoscopes seem to transfer similar, but less politically motivated, concerns about the individual, and necessarily, as well, the connection between the celestial and the terrestrial now focused upon the individual person. It is tempting to see in the emergence of personal astrology evidence of a change in the relation conceived between the individual and the cosmos, or the individual and the gods, after the mid-first millennium. Whether this is the case, and what relation it may have to the politics of the Achaemenid and even the Seleucid era, is subject to further inquiry, but not on the basis of the horoscope texts alone. These texts are far too laconic, and far too few to penetrate much further into the philosophical or religious commitment behind the Babylonian personal astrology.

The analysis of the Babylonian horoscopes from the point of view of their cultural and historical context belongs to a future study, in which the horoscopes can be viewed in the light of the traditions of Babylonian celestial divination as well as of astronomy, both non-mathematical and mathematical. In spite of their implicit purpose to prognosticate aspects of the life of the native, the ostensive astronomical nature of the genre ties the horoscopes together with diaries, almanacs, goal-year texts, ephemerides and procedure texts as sources for our reconstruction of the repertoire of Babylonian astronomy in the late first millennium.

The present edition focuses on the philological aspects of the corpus and the dating of the horoscopes by means of their astronomical content. The primary purpose of this work is to edit and translate the Babylonian horoscopes, but it is also hoped that this edition will contribute to the foundation for further study of Babylonian celestial divination and genethlialogy currently being laid by the publication of other cuneiform celestial omen and related texts. It is only on the basis of such a foundation that a meaningful comparison with Greek astrology may be undertaken by those competent to evaluate the vast literature in that field.

CHAPTER 1

NATURE AND CULTURAL CONTEXT
OF THE
BABYLONIAN HOROSCOPES

§1. Definition of the Genre

In view of prevailing assumptions about horoscopes, both historical (Greco-Roman or European) and modern, it would be well to begin the present study of cuneiform "horoscopes" by defining the particular nature of the Babylonian texts, thereby clarifying their differences from other texts also termed "horoscopes." Although the term itself derives ultimately from the Greek ὡροσκόπος (Latin *horoscopum*), certain concepts regarding the spherical universe, the ecliptic, the zodiacal signs, planetary influences, and methods of relating astronomical elements to both physical and psychic elements of an individual, all associated with horoscopic astrology in Greco-Roman antiquity, must not be assumed *a priori* to find counterparts in the Babylonian texts.[1]

Babylonian "horoscopes" are documents that assemble and record a particular series of astronomical data which have been determined to occur either on or near the date of the birth of an individual. A number of

---

[1] Extensive literature on Greco-Roman astrology cannot be given in a footnote. One can start with O. Neugebauer and H.B. van Hoesen, *Greek Horoscopes* (Philadelphia: American Philosophical Society, 1959); Dorotheus of Sidon, *Carmen Astrologicum*, ed. D. Pingree (Leipzig: Teubner, 1976); Hephaestion of Thebes, *Apotelesmatica* (Prognostics), ed. D. Pingree (Leipzig: Teubner, 1973); Vettius Valens, *Anthologiae*, ed. D. Pingree (Leipzig: Teubner, 1986); Manilius, *Astronomica*, ed. and transl. G.P. Goold (Cambridge, Mass., and London: Loeb Classical Library, 1977); Ptolemy, *Tetrabiblos*, ed. and transl. F.E. Robbins (Cambridge, Mass., and London: Loeb Classical Library, 1940); A. Bouché-Leclercq, *L'astrologie grecque* (Paris: Leroux, 1899), and D.Pingree, "Astrology," in P.P. Wiener ed., *Dictionary for the History of Ideas* Vol. I (New York: Scribner, 1968, 1973), pp. 118-126.

examples "look at the hour," noting the time of birth occasionally with respect to a seasonal hour (one-twelfth of the length of daylight),[2] and provide planetary positions in the zodiac for the specified time. Only the moon's position is affected by a change in hour, since it moves so much more rapidly than the sun or the five planets. That planetary data are not greatly affected, may perhaps explain why the hour of birth is not noted with regularity in the Babylonian horoscopes. Even when noted, the Babylonian horoscopes' "inspection of the hour" is not paralleled by their synonymous Greek counterparts, where ὡροσκόπος refers not to the consideration of the time of day, but of the point of the ecliptic (the ascendant) rising at the moment of birth (Ptolemy, *Tetrabiblos* III,2).

The differences between Babylonian and Greek horoscopes begin here and permeate most other aspects of the two corpora. Despite the evidence of transmission and borrowing from Mesopotamia found in specific elements of Greek astrology,[3] and that the basic idea of predicting the life of a person on the basis of astronomical phenomena associated with the birth date was originally Babylonian, Babylonian and Greek horoscopes reflect substantially different genethlialogical systems. There is neither chronological overlap between the two corpora,[4] nor any similarity between their underlying cosmologies or their philosophical/religious underpinnings. Mention should also be made of the Demotic horoscopes of Roman Egypt, dating to the first half of the first century A.D. and reflecting a Greco-Egyptian, rather than a Babylonian, foundation.[5] Parts of the composition of these horoscopes are formally similar to the Babylonian texts, e.g., the date of birth stated in terms of regnal year, month, day and hour, and the positions of the sun, moon, and planets, but the other elements included have no Babylonian analogues. On this basis, we proceed in the hopes that the term "horoscope" will not lead to a misunderstanding of the nature of the Babylonian examples, or of their cultural

---

[2] See chapter 3 § 2.3.3.

[3] See my "Elements of the Babylonian Contribution to Hellenistic Astrology," JAOS 108 (1987), pp. 51-62.

[4] The latest dated cuneiform horoscope is for S.E.243 = -68 = 69 B.C., the earliest Greek horoscope is the coronation monument for Antiochus I of Commagene in -61 = 62 B.C.. This is not a nativity but rather an "omen" for the reign of the king (much like the citing of auspicious planetary appearances by Esarhaddon at the beginning of his reign and recorded in his royal inscriptions, see Riekele Borger, *Die Inschriften Asarhaddons Königs von Assyrien* [Graz, 1956], p.2 i 31-ii 26 and p.17 lines 34-41). Even the Egyptian horoscopes date between -37 and +93. See Neugebauer and van Hoesen, *Greek Horoscopes*, p. 161.

[5] O. Neugebauer, "Demotic Horoscopes," JAOS 63 (1943), pp. 116-126.

background, by simple association with the Greek or their derivatives.

The discovery of the first cuneiform horoscope came as part of the general decipherment of astronomical cuneiform texts in the late nineteenth century by J. Epping, J.N. Strassmaier, and F.X. Kugler. At that time, in 1888, only a single horoscope text was known (Text 18).[6] Two more horoscopes were published in the 1920s,[7] but it was not until the 1960s that more examples were identified by Abraham Sachs in the British Museum. Twenty-eight Babylonian horoscope tablets are now extant. In the context of cuneiform scientific texts, this group may be seen as a well-defined class of astrological texts belonging to the Achaemenid, Seleucid, and Arsacid periods, or roughly between the fifth and first centuries B.C. Their content is ostensibly astronomical rather than "astrological," as practically no prognostications for the native are included in these documents.

The chronological range of the extant texts is from 410 B.C. to 69 B.C. The five documents from the first century B.C. are among the youngest cuneiform texts known. These first century horoscopes (Texts 23-27), all from the city of Babylon, date from the end of the reign of Mithradates II (88 B.C.) to 69 B.C., a period of political instability in Babylon, during which time Babylon's major temple, the Esagila, begins to appear moribund.[8]

The Babylonian horoscopes were all dated to the birth of an individual. Since three texts contain more than one horoscope, it cannot be the case that a horoscope was written on the date of the birth. In no case has the writing of a horoscope tablet been dated by means of a colophon. The dates are found at the beginning of the text and refer exclusively to the birth date. Given the existence of birth notes, recording dates and times of births apparently for the purpose of later casting a horoscope, it is clear that horoscopes could have been prepared well after such dates. In the single birth note preserved with more than one birth record, two of the dates are spaced thirty-six years. The evidence that data were excerpted from other astronomical texts further precludes the possibility that a

---

[6] Published by Strassmaier, ZA 3 (1888), p. 149f (transcription on p. 137) and Epping, ZA 4 (1889), pp. 168-171; also Kugler SSB II 554-558, and republished together with Text 7 (BM 33667) by Kugler, SSB II 558-562 (transliteration, translation and commentary) and Schaumberger, SSB Erg. 3 Tf.VII Nr. 14 (copy) (1924).

[7] Text 2 (AB 251) was published by R.C. Thompson, *A Catalogue of the Late Babylonian Tablets in the Bodleian Library*, Oxford (London: Luzac, 1927), pl.2. Text 7 by Kugler and Schaumberger, see note 6.

[8] J. Oelsner, *Materialien zur babylonischen Gesellschaft und Kultur in hellenistischer Zeit* (Budapest, 1986), p. 65.

horoscope represents some observation, or even computation, of heavenly phenomena at the time of birth.

§2. CONTENT AND PURPOSE OF THE GENRE

As records of astronomical phenomena, the Babylonian horoscopes are sources for the techniques, and indirectly, the intellectual or social context, of those who wrote them. Of the ultimate goal of the construction of these documents, the good and bad fortunes of the recipients, they tell us little. Still less is known from the texts about the individual recipients themselves. The historical problem of astrological interpretation seems to be endemic to the history of astrology on a broad scale, as expressed in a comment by J.D. North: "Historians faced with a nativity are almost always inclined to ask how it would have been interpreted. The answer is usually 'As its subject would have wished'."[9]

The purpose of the Babylonian horoscope document was above all to record positions of the seven planets (moon, sun, and five classical planets) in the zodiac on the date of a birth. The astronomical data were presented following a standard formulation:

> ITI.MN 30/1 GE$_6$ n *šerru alid*
> "MN, (the previous month being) full/hollow, night of
> the nth, the child was born."[10]

The majority of horoscopes do not name the child for whom the horoscope is cast, and simply use the phrase *šerru alid* "the child is born." In seven horoscopes (Texts 2, 4, 9, 12, and the duplicates 10 and 11,) and one birth note (Text 30), the name of the child is recorded. Two of these contain Greek personal names: Aristokrates, written *a-ri-is-tu-ug-gi-ra-te-e*,[11] and Nikanor, written *nik-nu-ú-ru*;[12] Both of these horoscopes date from the early third century, thus securely within a hellenized Babylonia. Even so, the Greek names may or may not represent ethnic Greeks, and conclusions as to the nationality of any of those for whom horoscopes were cast cannot yet be drawn.

---

[9]   J.D. North, *Horoscopes and History* (= Warburg Institute Surveys and Texts XIII, London: The Warburg Institute, University of London, 1986), p. xi.

[10]   For this formulation of the month, see chapter 3 § 2.2.

[11]   Text 10 obv. 2.

[12]   Text 12 obv. 2.

Inferences regarding the individuals involved in personal astrology may only be ventured about those who wrote the horoscopes, and this too is indirect and based exclusively on internal textual criteria, rather than on any data directly concerning the horoscope scribes. Primarily because the vocabulary of the horoscopes is the same as that of the Late Babylonian astronomical texts, both mathematical and non-mathematical, one may guess that they were produced by the same group of scribes. Precious little is known of these individuals, but from astronomical text colophons we do have names, patronyms, and professions for some of the hellenistic Babylonian astronomers.[13] A number of Arsacid period administrative documents from the Marduk temple Esagila of Babylon make reference to the scribes who specialized in celestial matters, calling them "scribes of (the celestial omen series entitled) *Enūma Anu Enlil*," and describing specific astronomical work for which they received support in the form of arable land and silver.[14] These temple documents clarify the association of the scribes of *Enūma Anu Enlil* with the temple during the second century B.C. and indicate that the activities of these scribes included observational and computational astronomy. Their duties regarding celestial divination, not to speak of horoscopy, are not referred to in the temple documents. It can only be assumed that since copies of *Enūma Anu Enlil* continued to be made during the hellenistic period, it was this same group of scribes who made them. Even on the basis of such scanty evidence as this, it is perhaps sufficient to say that the group of scribes known as *ṭupšar Enūma Anu Enlil* produced the horoscope tablets, as well as any other text of astronomical or astrological content, and that throughout the Achaemenid, Seleucid, and Arsacid periods these scribes belonged to an extremely small set of Babylonian literati.

Beyond their small numbers, evidence is wanting for the social standing of such scribes, and even less is available for their horoscope clients. The Greek names of two horoscopes can point to the Macedonian elite of late Babylonian society, but not unequivocally. In only one horoscope (Text 9) can the native named in the horoscope be identified. In this case, the subject was a scribe well-known from colophons in Hellenistic texts from

---

[13] The evidence is collected in my "Scribes and Scholars: The *ṭupšar Enūma Anu Enlil*," FS Oelsner (in press).

[14] See Pinches, BOR 4 132, CT 49 144, CT 44 186, and AB 247, published by McEwan in *Iraq* 43 (1981), pp. 139-141, and see the discussion in R.J. van der Spek, "The Babylonian Temple during the Macedonian and Parthian Domination," BiOr 42 (1985), pp. 547-554. The letters CT 49 189 and 192 contain references to the title *ṭupšar Enūma Anu Enlil*, but in broken context.

Uruk: Anu-bēlšunu, son of Nidintu-Anu, descendant of Sin-lēqe-unninni.[15] That a horoscope was cast for a member of a family of scholars and priests of the Anu temple of Uruk, suggests only that scribes could construct their own (or each others') horoscopes. It is no reflection on the accessibility of horoscopy for clients outside the circle of the scholars themselves. If, however, Babylonian horoscopy is to be understood as an extension of the traditional scholarly celestial divination, which above all served the king,[16] then it might be the case that the new form of celestial prognostication was confined to citizens of privilege. [17]Our evidence is, however, not sufficient to draw conclusions about the social dimension of late Babylonian astrology.

Following the date of the birth is the time of birth. More often than not the time is given with respect to a part of the day, e.g., *ina* ZALÁG "in the last part of night"[18] or SAG GE$_6$ "beginning of night."[19] The time of birth is also given with respect to the seasonal hours, the twelve divisions of the day whose number remain fixed but whose lengths vary throughout the year. The *simanu*, as they were called, are designated by ordinal numbers

---

[15] See Text 9 obv. 2.

[16] Note also that the physiognomic omens (eg. YOS 10 54), which have been found to be internally related to nativity omens (and perhaps horoscopes) insofar as their predictions for individuals are concerned, address the elite in society. Apodoses from the physiognomic series contain subject matter that points to the palace and its personnel, see for example YOS 10 54:22, 23, 30 and 31.

[17] Many basic aspects of the social structure of first millennium Babylonia, such as the social and economic "classes," are still to be fully understood, as attested to in statements such as M. Dandamaev, *Slavery in Babylonia: From Nabopolassar to Alexander the Great* (626-331 B C), transl. V.A. Powell (DeKalb: Northern Illinois University Press, rev.ed., 1984), pp.44-46; J. Klima, "Beiträge zur Struktur der neubabylonischen Gesellschaft, "CRRAI 11 (Leiden, 1964), pp. 11-21; see also the remarks concerning the status of "free citizen" (mār bānûti) in M. Roth, "A Case of Contested Status," in *DUMU, E$_2$-DUB-BA-A- Studies in honor of Åke W. Sjöberg* (Occasional Publications of the Samuel Noah Kramer Fund, 11, Philadelphia, 1989), pp. 486-487. In this context, to attach anything more than vague social significance to the prosopographical evidence from the horoscopes would be premature. Note however, that a connection between astrology and the ruler continued in the context of Hellenistic Greek horoscopy. A practice of preparing a horoscope for the coronation of a monarch is attested three times. One is the huge monument that represents in stone relief the earliest preserved horoscope. It can be dated to the coronation of Antiochus I of Commagene in 62 B.C., and is published in Neugebauer and van Hoesen, *Greek Horoscopes*, pp. 14-16. For the other examples, see ibid., p. 16 note 13.

[18] See Text 1:1, Text 19:4, and Text 20:2.

[19] See Text 6 rev. 2, Text 7 rev. 2, Text 13:2, Text 15:2, and Text 17:2.

(i.e. 7 *si-man* = the 7th *simanu*).[20] Elsewhere, *simanu* has the basic meaning "interval,"[21] but here the twelve intervals represent the twelve divisions of daylight or night (not the 12-*bēru* division of the nycthe-meron), and were used to denote the time of birth.[22] The enumeration of the planetary positions usually follow the expression "in his hour (of birth)" (*ina simaniŝu*).

The body of the horoscope contains the planetary positions in the zodiac. These data may follow several introductory expressions, e.g., "at that time" (*inūŝu*), "in his hour (of birth),"(*ina simaniŝu*), or "that day" (*ūmiŝu*). Then in a standard formulation, the planetary positions are given as follows: "the moon was in zodiacal sign$_x$, the sun was in zodiacal sign$_y$, Jupiter in zodiacal sign$_z$," followed by the positions of Venus, Mercury, Saturn, and Mars. These positions are generally given with respect to a zodiacal sign alone, less often in specific degrees within a sign. With several exceptions,[23] horoscopes do not generally record positions of planetary synodic phenomena, but rather positions in the zodiac at the arbitrary moment of someone's birth. When, however, a planet is in conjunction with the sun and is therefore not visible, the text notes that the planet has "set" (ŠÚ = *rabû*) and/or is "with the sun" (KI *Šamáš*= *itti Šamŝi*).[24]

§3. ANCIENT DERIVATION OF DATA

The question of the derivation of the astronomical data in the horoscopes is directly relevant to the question of the relationship between "astrology" and "astronomy" in Babylonia. Neugebauer drew attention to the fact that the Babylonian horoscopes constitute a very small corpus compared with the over 1800 late Babylonian astronomical texts.[25] Were it not for the wealth of astronomical data, and the resulting access to Babylonian astronomical techniques afforded by the astronomical texts, we would have little chance of identifying the methods by which astronomical data were derived in Babylonian horoscopes.

The relevance especially of the non-mathematical astronomical texts for analysis of the horoscopes is *prima facie* evident from the technical termin-

---

[20] E.g., Text 21:2'.

[21] See CAD s.v., ACT glossary s.v.

[22] See my "Seasonal Hours in Babylonian Astronomy," *Centaurus* 32 (1989), pp. 146-170.

[23] See Text 1 throughout, 4:6-7, 6 upper edge 2; 7 obv.(?) 2-3, 23:6, 25:7-8, and 28 rev. 2.

[24] See ch.2, Introduction to the text editions sub 3b.

[25] Neugebauer-van Hoesen, *Greek Horoscopes*, p. 162.

ology, as well as the orthographic conventions, employed by the writers of the horoscopes. The writings of all the key ingredients, that is, the months, zodiacal signs, names of planets and stars, designations of time and celestial positions, as well as terms for phenomena are familiar from other astronomical genres.[26] Several abbreviations, such as *ád* for *adriš* "darkly,"[27] *al* for *alla* "more than,"[28] and *ár* for *arki* "after,"[29] are also diag-nostic of the vocabulary and orthography of late Babylonian astronomy. This purely philological aspect of the horoscopes is sufficient to place the genre in its correct scholastic context, i.e., as fully part of the astronomical activities practiced by late Babylonian temple scholars.

The identification of data and methods of derivation, however, are not as straightforward as one might like. To begin with, the daily positions, so important to a horoscope, were not a primary goal of Babylonian planetary theory. At least as we know it from the mathematical ephemerides, the chief goal was the computation of dates and positions of the synodic phenomena. Tables of daily motion do exist for Jupiter[30] and Mercury,[31] where the longitudes of these planets are tabulated day-by-day, and the days of the month given for the planetary positions are real calendar days, not tithis (the unit 1/30 of a month, or, the lunar day). The purpose of these ephemerides is not really known, but Neugebauer has suggested that the astrologically important question of a planet's crossing from one zodiacal sign to the next may have provided a motivation.[32] Certainly, no evidence in the astronomical or astrological literature suggests that degrees within zodiacal signs were ever observed, and it may well have been the only solution to the problem of knowing when a planet would enter the next sign of the zodiac. Such daily ephemeris tables could conceivably have been of use in constructing horoscopes, but one can do no more than speculate about this since no reference to such a purpose, or to any other astrologically important configuration of planets, is found in procedure texts, or anywhere else. Moreover, daily positions for Venus, Saturn and

---

[26] See chapter 2, Introduction to the text editions, passim, for examples of the uniformity between the terminology of the horoscopes and the non-mathematical astronomical texts.

[27] Text 27 r.7.

[28] Text 27 r.6.

[29] Text 1:3; Text 6 r.2, and Text 14:3.

[30] ACT 650-655, and see P. Huber, "Zur täglichen Bewegung des Jupiter nach babylonischen Texten," ZA 18(1957), pp. 265-303.

[31] ACT 310.

[32] HAMA p.412.

Mars, which do occur in horoscopes, are not preserved in Seleucid ephemerides, although such positions could certainly have been derived by methods known for interpolation.[33] Astronomical procedure texts attest to such linear interpolation from the ephemerides, indicating that positions of planets on dates in between synodic apppearances were desired.

Whether or not such interpolation was the method employed in horoscopes for obtaining longitudes of planets on dates between their synodic appearances cannot be decided. But it is certain that the planetary data found in the horoscopes were the results either of some method of direct computation or, more likely, of extracting such data from other records. In his discussion of the non-mathematical astronomical texts' use of the zodiac, Sachs said, "An inspection of all the items that mention a sign of the zodiac shows that we are in the presence of predictions in all such cases. Because all the twelve signs of the zodiac are of equal length by definition, they constituted for the Babylonians an ideal system of reference for making longitude predictions, though it was probably beyond the capacity of Babylonian techniques of observational measurement to define in a precise way the boundary lines between the zodiacal signs in the sky."[34] Since planetary positions cited in Babylonian astronomical texts where the zodiac is used as the system of celestial reference do not represent observed positions, it is the case by extension that such positions in the horoscopes do not represent observations either.

Aside from the non-observational nature of the planetary phenomena, another general remark may be made about the planetary positions given in the horoscopes; namely, that the sequence in which they are given, Jupiter, Venus, Mercury, Saturn, Mars, is the standard sequence employed in the non-tabular astronomical texts of the Seleucid period, specifically almanacs and goal year texts, but also attested sporadically in much earlier texts. There has been much discussion about this peculiar sequence of planets for which there is no "natural" explanation, such as distance from the sun. What can now be substantiated with evidence from nativity omens of the same period is that this arrangement of planets stems from an astrological schema which assigns the planets beneficent and maleficent

---

[33] In HAMA, p. 465. Neugebauer commented, regarding the procedure text ACT 812 Sections 11-29 for Venus, that "were it fully preserved [it] would give us all data for the 'subdivision' of the synodic motion." For Mars, the procedure text ACT 811 Section 3, he says (HAMA, p. 456), "is explicit evidence for the use of the principle of proportionality between synodic arcs ω_i and corrections for approximate periods , similarly established for the periods of Jupiter." Daily positions could be found by means of such texts.

[34] Sachs, "A Classification of the Babylonian Astronomical Tablets of the Seleucid Period," *JCS* 2 (1948): p. 289.

identities, possibly on the basis of brightness.[35]The Babylonian arrangement of the planets can therefore be analyzed as the benefic pair Jupiter
and Venus followed by Mercury which is sometimes benefic, sometimes
ambiguous, and lastly the malefic pair Saturn and Mars.[36] The same
identifications, in fact, became a commonplace in later Hellenistic
astrology.[37] The identification of the planets as benefic or malefic, while
assured on the basis of nativity omen texts, cannot, however, be derived
directly from the horoscopes themselves, since these texts give only the
results of the computations of planetary positions on the date in question,
without reference to the interpretation of the phenomena recorded. The
arrangement of the planets in the horoscopes, as well as in Babylonian
astronomy in general, consequently bears no relation to a concept of where
the heavenly bodies are located in the sky. This is contrasted in the Greek
horoscopes, which provide much the same data as do the Babylonian
counterparts, but list the planetary positions in order of their distances
from the earth, thereby reflecting their spatial location in a geocentric
cosmos. The Greek order is Saturn, Jupiter, Mars, Venus and Mercury
(having the same sidereal period), in descending order of their periods of
sidereal rotation, hence their geocentric distance.[38]

   In addition to the positions of the planets on the date of birth, other

---

[35] See my "Benefics and Malefics in Babylonian Astrology," in *A Scientific Humanist: Studies in Memory of Abraham Sachs*, ed. Leichty, et al (Occasional Publications of the Samuel Noah Kramer Fund 9, Phila., PA, 1988), pp. 323-328.

[36] Evidence for the assignment of planetary "natures" is for the most part not explicit, but subtly reflected in the interpretation of the appearances of individual planets. The most explicit evidence is in some of the names and epithets of Mars, the quintessentially "evil planet," who was, in addition, associated with the god of pestilence and death, Nergal. Mars was called MUL.LUL.LA (*sarru*) "Liar (star)" and MUL.LÚ.KÚR.RA (*nakru*) "Enemy (star),"see Hg.B VI 33-34 in MSL 11 40. In the same text is also the name MUL.HUL (*lumnu*) "Evil fate (star)," Hg. B VI 30, see CAD s.v. *lumnu* lexical section.

[37] The hellenistic doctrines are discussed by D. Pingree, *The Yavanajātaka of Sphujidhvaja* vol. II (Harvard Oriental Series 48, Cambridge, Mass., and London: Harvard University Press, 1978), pp. 214-215.

[38] The Greek horoscopes, which are all late Hellenistic (none outside the literary sources antedates 4 B.C.), follow the order of the planets by geocentric distance, but as Neugebauer has shown, the chronology of Greek planetary sequences is not a simple evolution, and the bases on which the sequences are proposed are variously mythological, numerological, arithmetical, or astronomical, meaning based on cinematic planetary models. The ascription of a geocentric distance arrangement to Plato, based upon Timaeus 38 D, is not evidence of Greek knowledge of such a sequence in the fifth century, especially with regard to the relative positions of Venus and Mercury. See HAMA pp. 647-651, 690-693, and 785.

astronomical events of the month or even the year in which the birth occurred are frequently appended. Horoscopes record the following lunar phenomena: Whether the month was full (30^d) or hollow (29^d), the date of the time interval termed NA (=*nanmurtu*) around full moon, usually on the 14th day, which measured the interval between sunrise and moonset, and the date of another time interval of last lunar visibility before sunrise termed KUR.[39] These three data—length of the month, *na* and KUR—are what Sachs termed the "lunar three."[40] The lunar three are found in each monthly paragraph of an astronomical almanac, and are obtainable in diaries and other types of non-mathematical texts of the Seleucid period. Besides the lunar three, horoscopes record lunar and solar eclipses, including those not observed or visible at Babylon; the conjunctions of the moon with the ecliptical reference stars (termed normal stars); as well as the dates of equinoxes and solstices for the given year. Statements about lunar latitude are included in three horoscopes from Uruk, although this should probably be regarded as rare.[41]

§4. RELIGIOUS AND DIVINATORY CONTEXT

Apart from the content of a typical horoscope relevant to the astronomical positions on the birthdate, a number of horoscopes contain another element shared by other astronomical texts. This is the formulaic invocation to the deities associated either with the temples of Babylon or Uruk, i.e., Bēl and Bēltīja for Babylon, Anu and Antum for Uruk: *ina amat Bēl u Bēltīja lišlim* or *ina amat Anu u Antum lišlim* . The translation of the invocation is subject to some interpretation regarding the verb *šalāmu*, which can either mean "to be whole," referring to the tablet, or "to be successful," referring to the endeavor of writing the tablet. The few texts which preserve a longer version of the prayer would suggest the latter interpretation, for example, *ina amat Anu u Antum mimma mala eppuš ina qātēja lišlim* "by the command of Anu and Antu, may whatever I do be

---

[39] The oppositions (computed by means of NA) and conjunctions (computed by means of KUR), for which the length of the month would be needed, are the data needed for computing the time of conception (D. Pingree, personal communication). Further research is needed before the use of the date of conception versus that of birth in Babylonian astrology is understood. It is clear, though, that omens for the date of conception were compiled, see for example, LBAT 1588 and 1589 (LÚ.TUR *re-ḫi*).

[40] A. Sachs, "A Classification of the Babylonian Astronomical Tablets of the Seleucid Period," *JCS* 2 (1948): p. 278.

[41] See Texts 10 and 16a and b.

successful."[42] The other possibility is that the referent is the tablet itself. In this case, the aim of the prayer would be that the tablet should remain unbroken or safe in its repository. This interpretation finds support in colophons which curse the removal or damage of a tablet.[43] The formula is known exclusively in Seleucid texts, but from a range of text genres, including literature (*Lugale*[44]), magic,[45] divination,[46] astronomy,[47] legal documents,[48] and an isolated administrative text.[49]

On the evidence of extant temple archives, mainly from the *Esagila* in Babylon and the *Bīt Rēš* in Uruk, one can affirm that in the protective atmosphere of the temple, Mesopotamian religion, scholarship, and science continued until the first century A.D.[50] It is in this context that we must understand the invocation to Bēl and Bēltija in the Babylonian astronomical texts—including horoscopes—, and to Anu and Antu in those from Uruk, discussed above. Association with the temple was without doubt the key to the survival of Babylonian astronomy for so many centuries after it had become defunct in the political sphere. As a further consequence, the maintenance of Babylonian astronomy and astrology by the temple scholars made possible its transmission to literate Greeks

---

[42] TCL 6 31, a mathematical text from Seleucid Uruk, with a parallel from Babylon, SBH 14. Other texts with variants include BRM 4 8 and Bagh. Mitt. Beiheft 2 No.12, edited by Mayer, "Seleucidische Rituale aus Warka mit Emesal-Gebeten," *Orientalia* NS 47 (1978): pp. 431-58. M.T. Roth has collected the data in "*ina amat* DN$_1$ *u* DN$_2$ *lišlim*," *Journal of Semitic Studies* 33 (1988): pp. 1-9.

[43] Hunger *Kolophone* No.319, 320, or 333. See also G. Offner, "A propos de la sauvegarde des tablettes en Assyro-Babylonie," *RA* 44 (1950), pp. 135-43. For the entreaty not to damage a tablet, see *āmiru la itappil* "let the reader not damage it (the tablet)," in A. Livingstone, *Mystical and Mythological Explanatory Works of Assyrian and Babylonian Scholars* (Oxford: Clarendon Press, 1986), p. 28f. K 2670 colophon line 9 (=I.NAM.GIŠ.HUR.AN.KI.A).

[44] See Hunger *Kolophone* No. 87.

[45] Ibid. No. 425.

[46] Ibid. No.95, from the *bārûtu* series.

[47] See ACT I pp.11 and 16.

[48] See Roth, "*ina amat* DN$_1$ *u* DN$_2$ *lišlim*," p. 1.

[49] NBC 8456:1, see P.-A. Beaulieu, "Textes Administratifs Inedits d'Epoque Hellenistique Provenant des Archives du Bīt Rēš," RA 83 (1989), pp. 79-80 (Text 5).

[50] See A. Sachs, "The Last Dateable Cuneiform Texts," Kramer Anniversary Volume, *Alter Orient und Altes Testament* 25 (Neukirchen, 1976), pp. 379-398.

interested in the science of "ancient wise men, that is the Chaldeans."[51]

Despite their unique form and purpose, the Babylonian horoscopes can be seen as belonging to the broader tradition of Mesopotamian celestial divination for the simple reason that "apodoses," recognizable from omen texts, are the form taken by the few attested statements concerning the life of the native in horoscope texts. [52] All but two examples containing such apodoses stems from Uruk.[53] The evidence is found largely in broken context, but some of what is preserved can be associated with stock phrases from extispicy as well as the daily life omen series known as *Šumma ālu* and hemerological omen texts. These phrases, such as *ūmēšu arkū* "his days (i.e., his life) will be long" (Text 9:4; cf. Text 10:8), *mārū irašši* "he will have offspring" (Text 9:6; cf. Text 10:10), or *nēmela immar* "he will see a gain" (Text 5 rev. 10), parallel omen apodoses in form as well as content.

The tradition of celestial omens was many centuries old at the point when horoscopic astrology began, i.e., by the end of the fifth century on the basis of the evidence of our earliest horoscopes.[54] Copies of the series *Enūma Anu Enlil*, the scholars' handbook used during the seventh century to advise the Neo-Assyrian kings Esarhaddon and Assurbanipal, continued to be reproduced throughout the Achaemenid and Seleucid periods. This is clear from *Enūma Anu Enlil* text colophons or, when not preserved, the characteristic late ductus of the script.[55] For the periods of Persian and Macedonian political rule, however, evidence for the practice of celestial divination is limited to the scholars' efforts to preserve and transmit the traditional texts. No letters such as those from the Sargonid period, from scholar-scribes to kings of this late period attest to the practice of celestial divination at court. The preservation of the *Enūma Anu Enlil* reference work by generations of scribes from roughly the fifth to the first centuries B.C., therefore, has no evident political purpose.

The formulation of personal predictions in horoscopes, in the manner of omen apodoses, serves to indicate that the traditional practice of celestial divination, by means of which aspects of the life of the king and the welfare of the state had been indicated by celestial signs, provided the foundation, the basic rationale, and possibly also the system of interpreting

---

[51] Horoscope No. 137C col.i 3, see Neugebauer-van Hoesen, *Greek Horoscopes*, p.42.

[52] See chapter 3 § 4.2.

[53] Text 2 rev. 1, Text 5 rev. 1-12, Text 9:4-6, and Text 10: 7-9 and rev. 1-3, with duplicate Text 11.

[54] Texts 1 and 2.

[55] For some representative colophons of *Enūma Anu Enlil*, see H. Hunger Kolophone, Nos. 87, 91, and 93.

the life of an individual from the situation of the heavens at the moment of birth. To read the heavens as meaningful not only for the king and the state, but also for the individual, is evidenced both by late Babylonian horoscopes and by the roughly contemporaneous "nativity" omens.

One may differentiate, as Sachs suggested, two types of nativity omens. The "horoscopic" nativity omen correlated the zodiacal sign in which the person was born with positive or negative characteristics and experiences of the native, e.g., "if a child is born in the middle of Aries."[56] The other type made similar correlations between an individual's life and an astral phenomenon that occurred on the birthdate, e.g., "if a child is born and Jupiter comes forth,"[57] without mention of the zodiac. An example of a "horoscopic" nativity omen is LÚ.TUR *ina* MÚL.MÚL *a-lid* MÚL.GU₄. AN.NA ᵈ*A-nim* GAL-*ú šá* AN-*e* LÚ.BI SIG-*e* DUMU.MEŠ [*u*] DUMUxSAL.MEŠ GUR-*ar* Á.TUK IGI-[*mar*] "(If) a child is born in Taurus, the Bull of Heaven (is) Great Anu of heaven: That man will be distinguished, his sons and daughters will return and he will see gain." (BM 32224 ii 13'-15'). The following, on the other hand, are "pseudo-horoscopic": LÚ.TUR *a-lid-ma ina* GABA-*šú šamáš* KAxMI *ina* NU URU-*šú* BE É AD-*šú* BIR "(If) a child is born and during his infancy a solar eclipse occurs: He will die in a foreign city (lit.: in a city not his own) and the house of his father will be scattered." (BM 32488 obv. 10'); [LÚ.TUR ... *a-lid* ...] *ze-e-ri ina lib-bi-šu* GÁL-*ši* ... *a-di* 3 MU.AN.NA.MEŠ *mim-ma i-rak-kis ina* ŠUᴵᴵ-*šú* UL GUB-*zu* NÍG.ŠID *ra-ma-ni-šú i-rak-kis u ne-me-lu* IGI-*mar* "[A child is born and ...] there will be anger in his heart ... for 3 years whatever he takes(?) will not remain in his hands (meaning "he will lose what he has"?), (then) he will keep(?) his own property and will see a profit." (BM 32304 ii 6,8,9,10).

Sachs saw the difference between the "horoscopic" type, those mentioning zodiacal signs, and the "pseudo-horoscopic," which made no mention of the zodiac, as significant for the evolution of astrology. He suggested that the pseudo-horoscopic omens reflected a "pre-horoscopic level of development,"[58] but, in view of texts like TCL 6 14 where both types are combined in a single text, it is very difficult to be sure about such a sequence.

As scholastic forerunners to the nativity omen protases, the birth omens

---

[56] See the unpublished BM 32583 obv. i 16-17: DIŠ MURUB₄ HUN *a-lid* .... Á.TUK IGI-*mar* 2 DUMU.MEŠ-*šú* UŠ.MEŠ "If (the native) is born in the middle of Aries, ... he will see gain, (but) two of his sons will die."

[57] TCL 6 14, see Sachs, JCS 6 (1952), Appendix II, pp. 65-75.

[58] Ibid., p.73 in comments to obverse 27-36, and p. 74 in comments to reverse 29ff.

of the sort attested in the omen series *Iqqur īpuš* in the form "if a child is born on such-and-such a date" may also be cited.[59] These systems of determining from a calendar date something of relevance for an individual bear relation to the tradition of the menologies and hemerologies in which actions, such as marrying, laying the foundation of a house, or "going out the gate,"[60] on particular dates were determined to be propitious or unpropitious.[61] The apodoses of the nativity omens also find close parallels in the other major "personal" omen series, the physiognomic omens. [62]

We have assumed that the purpose of the Babylonian horoscopes, which produce a record of celestial phenomena at the time of a birth, was to obtain an indication about the life of an individual born on that date. The goal of these texts, therefore, is not substantially different from that of the nativity omens, although the method of obtaining the desired knowledge differs substantially. The examination of the situation of the heavens on the birth date, as it is formulated in the horoscopes, seems to be predicated on the idea, fully consistent with that of the omens, that knowledge about the world of human endeavor, here an individual's life, was encoded in the heavens. Unfortunately, little or no direct evidence of the system of astrological interpretation for individuals is available from the horoscopes themselves. They are, as outlined above, terse and laconic, usually stating only the date and the planetary positions for a particular birthdate. Without the few "predictions" in the form of omen apodoses occasionally included in horoscopes, the important connection between horoscopes and celestial divination would be lost.

The scholarly tradition underlying the development of horoscopy, therefore, can be seen as a combination of the tradition of celestial divination as represented by the omen series *Enūma Anu Enlil*, which always retained its concern with public matters (king and state), and the tradition of birth omens , whose apodoses pertained to the individual.

---

[59] See Labat *Calendrier*, p. 132f. § 64 (K.11082) for divination from the birth date of a child.

[60] Cf. similar omens for going out of the gate, *Babyloniaca* IV 202:27ff.

[61] S. Langdon, *Babylonian Menologies and the Semitic Calendars* (London, 1935), pp. 48-53 and 67-109. Other ancient Near Eastern parallels for birth omens based on date of birth are attested from Hittite as well as Egyptian sources. A Hittite fragment, translated from an Old Babylonian text derives predictions from the date of a child's birth, is cited by Oppenheim in "Man and Nature in Ancient Mesopotamia," *Dictionary of Scientific Biography* 15, p. 644; see also B. Meissner, "Über Genethlialogie bei den Babyloniern,"*Klio* 19 (1925, pp.432-434; also K. Riemschneider, *Studien zu den Boghazköy-Texten* 9 (Wiesbaden, 1970), p. 44 n.39a; and for an Egyptian parallel, see Bakir, *The Cairo Calendar No. 86637* (Cairo, 1966), especially pp. 13-50.

[62] F.R. Kraus, *Texte zur babylonischen Physiognomatik* (AfO Beiheft 3, Berlin, 1939).

These in turn share features with other omen genres, such as the physio-gnomic series or even some parts of the extispicy series, which contain apodoses beginning "that man" (*awīlu šū*) and continue with predictions for long life, wealth, family, etc. The nativity omens also combine these elements of the life of an individual together with celestial phenomena, either phenomena occurring at the time of the birth, such as the first visibility of a planet, or zodiacal signs, such as "the place of Leo: he will grow old (TCL 6 14 obv. 23)."

Since the predictions resulting from horoscopes were not substantially different from those of nativity omens, which generally concerned the person's economic status, number of heirs, and the like, it would appear that the situation of the heavens on the date of birth was interpreted as a collection of signs or celestial omens. As such, horoscopes would represent not an entirely new form of astrology, but a variant form of celestial divination, one formed from the synthesis of birth omina and the celestial omina of the kind compiled in the series *Enūma Anu Enlil*. Babylonian horoscopes are perhaps the extension and elaboration of nativity omens, but depend on a far more sophisticated astronomical apparatus than did the earlier tradition of celestial omens and nativity omens. Babylonian horoscopes and nativity omens may represent the end of the development of Mesopotamian genethlialogy, but they constitute the source of the genethlialogical branch of astrology that emerged in the Hellenistic Greek world.

CHAPTER 2:

INTRODUCTION TO TEXT EDITIONS

§ 1 PRESENTATION OF HOROSCOPES AND BIRTH NOTES

The texts in this edition are presented following the basic format of Sachs, "Babylonian Horoscopes," in JCS 6, which is: date and publication information, followed by transcription, critical apparatus, translation, and finally, commentary on the astronomical data. Among the possible conventional systems of transliterating cuneiform, I have adopted that of Sachs-Hunger, *Diaries*.

Dates have been established for the texts, or when a date is preserved, the dates are checked by means of planetary longitudes. These planetary longitudes are tabulated separately in the astronomical commentary to each horoscope, where the ancient data are compared against modern computed longitudes (see below chapter 2 §2.1 *Longitudes*). The longitude tables present three columns: the list of seven planets, their longitudes (or position with respect to a normal star) found in the horoscope, and their longitudes computed by modern means. Rarely are degrees of longitude given in the texts. Ecliptical longitude is generally expressed with respect to the name of a zodiacal sign. And when degrees of longitude are given, these too, in the standard manner of Babylonian astronomical texts, are expressed with reference to the 30 degrees of a zodiacal sign, i.e., not with reference to a continuous 360 degree ecliptic. The Babylonian zodiac was at all times sidereal (see this chapter below § 2.1). For comparison of the ancient and modern data, my computation, wherever possible, also takes into account a time of birth. The hour (or approximate time) of birth is determined either from direct statements in the text, or approximated on the basis of other internal evidence (such as the position of the moon). In the total absence of evidence, planetary positions were computed simply for the time just after sunset, i.e., the beginning of the Babylonian day.

For the most part, each document is a unique text and deals with a single horoscope. Standardization of form and content is evident on the level of the kinds of data and the order in which these are given. The specifics of each horoscope, however, obviously differ from one text to another. Only Texts 10 and 11 are duplicates. The purpose of a copy of a horoscope is unknown. Duplicates of other astronomical texts, such as

almanacs, are known to have been made as well.[1] One can perhaps find a
practical purpose in these multiple copies, providing an array of
astronomical data for an entire year. Why a copy of a horoscope might
have been made is not at all clear. Texts 6, 16, and 22 contain two
horoscopes each. The horoscopes recorded together on one tablet are
chronologically close, spaced by 7, 1, and 2 years respectively. Only one of
the three, however, exhibits any obvious relationship between the two
horoscopes, viz., Text 22, in which most of the planets were found in the
sign of Cancer (see commentary to Text 22 a and b). In these cases, the
question for whom the horoscopes were written poses itself. Given that
more than one horoscope could be combined on a single tablet, it seems
more likely that the documents were written not for the subject of the
horoscope, but for the interpreter. Our ignorance of the practical nature
of these documents does not warrant any further conclusions.

The texts are presented in chronological order, in accordance with
the dates of the births (see chapter 2 § 3.1 Text Catalogue), as these are not,
strictly speaking, dated documents. The changes in terminology (such as
terms for parts of the day, planet names, or astronomical phenomena), or
conventions of dating, concur with those observable in non-mathematical
astronomical texts. The horoscopes, therefore, do not appear as a genre
wholly apart from others of astronomical or astrological content. The less
than 30 extant horoscope tablets range chronologically from ca. 400 to ca.
50 B.C. The largest gap, of 112 years comes between texts 2 and 3. Table
2.1 below shows the sequence of dates. In the period for which 1800+
astronomical texts and a great many celestial omen tablets are preserved,
the paucity of horoscopes is difficult to interpret.[2] One possible
explanation is that the scribes who prepared and interpreted them kept the
tablets in their private archives, which have not been uncovered.[3] As far

---

[1] For example, the four copies of the almanac for 7/6 B.C., published by A.Sachs and C.B.F.
Walker, "Kepler's View of the Star of Bethlehem and the Babylonian Almanac for 7/6 B.C.,"
Iraq 46 (1984), pp.4-55.

[2] See Neugebauer-van Hoesen, *Greek Horoscopes*, p.162 where this is interpreted as no
accident.

[3] Only rarely has the personal "Fachbibliothek" of a scribe in late Babylonian times been
excavated. One such is that of the scribe Iqīšâ from Uruk, whose dated colophons place him
during the reign of Philipp Arrhidaeus, between 323 and 316 B.C. This scribe's archive was
excavated during the 27th, 29th, and 30th campaigns at Uruk, see von Weiher, UVB 29/30,
pp.96ff. and SpTU II. This scribe's profession was *āšipu* "exorcist," but he held tablets of
astronomical and astrological content as well as medical texts, incantations, and lexical lists.
Another small collection of tablets in a private residence at Uruk is tentatively connected
to the scribe Anu-ikṣur, see J. Schmidt, *XVI. und XXVII. vorläufiger Bericht über ... Uruk-
Warka 1968-1969* (Berlin, 1972), with discussion of the tablets by H. Hunger, pp. 79-87.

as the archive at Babylon from which the majority of the extant texts came, the unscientific nature of the excavation makes the reconstruction of that archive impossible.

The birth notes are not overtly astrological. They contain only the dates and times of births without reference to the heavens. Only one (Text 30) gives the name of the child, and there the formulation is parallel to that in a horoscope (Text 4 rev. 5). The attention to the specific moment of birth supports the connection to horoscopes as well. Text 32 includes three birthdates and times. From texts such as these, that provide the year, month, date, and time of day, horoscopes could be computed.

§ 2 METHODS OF DATING

§ 2.1 *Longitudes*

The horoscopes are not dated documents in the sense that the time of writing of the document is given. The date of birth, which is the key item, is given in all cases, but unfortunately is not always preserved. In most cases, establishing the date of the horoscope is a matter of finding the closest fit between the ancient planetary longitudes given in the text and longitudes obtained through modern computation. To compare modern computed longitudes against those in a Babylonian source it is helpful to correct for a systematic deviation in values that results from the different methods of counting longitude, i.e., modern tropical versus Babylonian sidereal longitudes.[4] This systematic deviation represents the effect of precession upon the sidereally normed Babylonian zodiac.

For the modern computed values, both for planetary positions and eclipses, I have utilized a program designed by P. Huber for the p.c. (Planets, Lunec, and Solec). After obtaining modern tropical longitudes from Planets, I adjusted the values before tabulating them (see Astronomical Data following each text edition) by a correction factor for the date in question. The equivalence is

$$\lambda_{\text{Babylonian}} = \lambda_{\text{tropical}} + \Delta \lambda$$

and

---

[4] I am grateful to John P. Britton for his construction of the systematic correction procedure adopted here. It has proved extremely helpful when Babylonian longitudes are to be compared against those obtained by means of modern computation, as has been done in the text editions below. This procedure is based upon a correction factor stemming from P. Huber's determination of $4°28^1$ as the mean difference between ancient and modern λ's for the year –100, see Huber, "Über den Nullpunkt der babylonischen Ekliptik," *Centaurus* 5 (1958), pp. 192-208.

$$\Delta \lambda = 3.08° + 0.013825° \times \text{(year date number)}$$

where 3.08° is the correction factor for the year 0, 0.013825° is the constant of precession per 100 years, and the year date is always negative. The following table lists the correction factors used in preparing the tables of astronomical data following each text:

Table 2.1

Text	Year Date	Correction Factor
1	-409	8.73°
2	-409	8.73°
3	-297	7.18°
4	-287	7.04°
5	-262	6.70°
6a	-258	6.64°
7	-257	6.63°
6b	-250	6.53°
8	-250	6.53°
9	-248	6.50°
10	-234	6.31°
11	-234	6.31°
12	-229	6.24°
13	-223	6.16°
14	-219	6.10°
15	-201	5.85°
16b	-199	5.83°
16a	-198	5.81°
17	-175	5.49°
18	-141	5.02°
19	-139	5.00°
20	-125	4.80°
21	-124	4.79°
22a	-116	4.68°
22b	-114	4.65°
23	-87	4.12°
24	-82	4.21°
25	-80	4.18°
26	-75	4.11°
27	-68	4.02°

It will be seen in the tabulated astronomical data following each text edition, that the Babylonian longitudes, obtained by a variety of methods observations such as were available in the diaries), appear remarkably correct. However, the apparent precision created by setting modern values, computed to hundreths of seconds of arc, against ancient values, most of which are given not to degrees within signs but by zodiacal sign alone, is something to be regarded with caution. Discrepancies between the ancient and modern longitudes, as revealed in the tabulated astronomical data following each horoscope, may be due to any number of causes, for example inaccuracies of dating, or in the absence of textual data, the need to base computation on approximate rather than actual time of birth. "Errors" of ± 1 or 2° in the Babylonian longitudes which seem to be inaccurate by our methods but which may be consistent with theirs are to be considered irrelevant, particularly inasmuch as we still cannot confidently identify the ancient methods used to obtain their results.

It is interesting to test those longitudes given with degrees in several horoscopes (Texts 5, 9, 10, 16 a and b, 21, 23, and 27) against modern computed longitudes. The following table summarizes this data. Please note that the values tabulated under column "λComputed" are rounded up to the nearest tenth degree.

Table 2.2

Text	Date	Time	λText	λComputed	Time	Δλ (λBab.-λmodern) [5]
5	-262 Apr.4	(last part of night)[6]	☉ ♈ 13.5°	16.28	4 UT	-2.8°
9	-248 Dec.29	evening	☉ ♐ 9.5°	281.8°	16 UT	-2.3°
			☾ ♒ 12°	315.39°		-3.4°
10	-234 Jun.2/3	dawn	☉ ♊ 12.5°	73.49°	1 UT	-1
			♃ ♐ 18°	260.05°		-2
			♀ ♉ 4°	27.85°		6.2°
			♄ ♋ 6°	90.48°		+5.5
			♂ ♋ 24°	115.6°		-1.6
16b	-199 Jun.5	dawn	☾ ♋ 15°	118.61°	1.75 UT	-13.6°
			♃ ♏ 26°	237.9°		-1.9°
			♀ ♊ 5°	62.4°		+2.6°
			☿ ♊ 27°	84.4°		+2.6°
			♄ ♍ 10°	157.2°		+2.8°
			♂ ♉ 10°	38.3°		+1.7°
16a	-198 Oct.31	dawn	♃ ♐ 10°	275.3°	3 UT	+4.7°

---

[5] The Δλ's reflect rounded values of the modern computed longitudes.

[6] The time of birth is not given in the text.

Table 2.2 continued

Text	Date	Time	λText	λComputed	Time	Δλ (λBab.-λmodern)
			♀ ♑ 4°	267.4°		+6.6°
			☿ ♏ 8°	227.7°		-9.7°
			♄ ♎ 3°	183.1°		0°
			♂ ♐ 10°	248°		+2°
21	-124 Oct.1	dawn	☾ ♋ 24°	113.5°	2 UT	+0.5°
	-124 Oct.2		☾ ♌ 9°	127.7°		+1.3°
23	-87 Jan. 5	midnight	☾ ♉ 5°	32.9°	21 UT	+2.1°
			♃ ♈ 27°	25.9°		1.1°
			♀ ♓ 1°	330.8°		0°
			☿ ♐ 26°	266.4°		0°
			♄ ♊ [20°]	79.4°		+0.6°
			♂ ♌ 20°	141.1°		-1.1°
27	-68 Apr.16	9th hr.	☾ ♑ 18°	297.8°	11.5 UT	-9.8°
			☉ ♈ 30°	27.5°		+2.5°
			♃ ♐ 24°	261.9°		+2.1°
			♀ ♊ 13°	72.7°		0°
			♄ ♒ 15°	314.2°		+0.8°
			♂ ♎ 14°	189.8°		+4.2°

Note that in Texts 16b and 27, the position of the moon indicates a discrepancy of approximately one day, suggesting that our data for the first day of the month is incorrect.

Table 2.3 shows planet-by-planet the differences (Δλ) between the Babylonian longitudes of the horoscopes containing degrees within zodiacal signs (data from table 2.2) and modern computed longitudes. A slash indicates an absence of data for the planet.

Table 2.3

Date	Text	Moon	Sun	Jupiter	Venus	Mercury	Saturn	Mars
-262	5	/	-2.8	/	/	/	/	/
-248	9	-3.4	+2.3	/	/	/	/	/
-234	10	/	-1	- 2	+6.2	/	+5.5	-1.6
-199	16b	-13.6	/	-1.9	+2.6	+2.6	+2.8	+1.7
-198	16a	/	/	+4.7	+6.6	-9.7	0	+2
-124	21	+0.5	/	/	/	/	/	/
-124	21	+1.3	/	/	/	/	/	/
-87	23	+2.1	/	+1.1	0	0	+0.6	-1
-68	27	-9.8	+2.5	+2.1	0	/	+0.8	+4.2

The large discrepancies in the computed longitudes for the moon (Texts 16b and 27) can reflect an error in the time used in computation, i.e., that it was not close enough to the time designated by the text, or that our data for the length of the month is in error by one day. The rather large deviations, close to the number of degrees that the moon moves (13°) per day, are suggestive of the latter. Taking into account this possibility for error in computation, the longitudes given in degrees within signs in the horoscopes, by and large, correlate very well with the positions obtained from modern computation. Implied is the excellence of the Babylonian methods of obtaining these longitudes.. Whether this points to the application of longitude schemes belonging to the mathematical astronomy, however, is another question. But apart from such schemes we know of no other source for obtaining longitudes expressed in degrees per sign.

§ 2.2 *Calendar Relationships*

As is customary in the dating of cuneiform texts, the correspondence betweeen Babylonian and the Julian calendars has been given in the dating of the horoscopes. Since the texts belong exclusively to years before A.D.1, the use of negative years (year [n+1] B.C. = -n) has been adopted as is conventional for astronomical chronology. Thus, -500 = 501 B.C., -99 = 100 B.C., and 0 = 1 B.C.

In accordance with the lunar calendar where the first day of the month begins with the sighting of the crescent moon just after sunset, the Babylonian day began at sunset. Therefore, Babylonian days, reckoned from sunset to sunset, fall between two consecutive civil days in the Julian calendar, which are reckoned from midnight to midnight. The correlation between Babylonian and Julian dates may be shown by the following figure in which B (Babylonian date) = J (Julian date)/J+1, SS = sunset, SR = sunrise, and mn = midnight.

Fig. 2.1

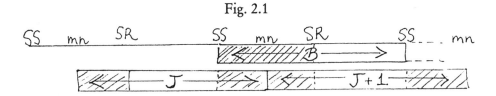

The convention of Parker-Dubberstein,[7] using the midnight epoch, correlates the Babylonian day with the Julian day that coincides with the

[7] R.A. Parker and W.H. Dubberstein, *Babylonian Chronology 626 B.C.-A.D.75* (Brown University Press, Providence, Rhode Island, 1956, 1971 4th ed.), pp.25-26.

daylight part of the Babylonian day, even though the beginning of the Babylonian day precedes this date by the time between sunset and midnight. Sachs-Hunger[8] correlate the Babylonian and Julian dates differently. They have given the equivalent dates for the beginning of Babylonian months by means of the correlation not between Babylonian day 1, but the preceding "day 0." They list the two consecutive Julian calendar dates that correspond to this day 0, and so Parker-Dubberstein dates for the beginning of the Babylonian months are $n_{\text{Sachs-Hunger}} + 1$, if one takes the second day from Sachs-Hunger. Dates for the horoscopes are restated in terms of the Julian calendar, either, in cases where the time of birth is indeterminable, by means of the two consecutive Julian dates that the Babylonian day overlaps, or, if the time of birth is known, by the Julian date that correlates with the part of the day on which the birth falls.

For the purpose of translating the time of birth and to compute the longitudes for the appropriate moment, the equivalent in Universal Time (UT) (=Greenwich Mean Time [GMT]) has been used in accordance with the conventions of other works of historical chronology based on astronomical computation, such as those of Tuckerman,[9] and Hunger-Dvorak.[10] The following time relationships apply: 0 GMT (also UT) = 12 midnight.
For geographic longitudes east of Greenwich,

$$\text{local time} = \text{GMT} + (\text{geographic longitude}°/15°)^{\text{hour}}$$

Because the geographical longitude of Babylon is 45° east of Greenwich at 0°, and every 15° = 1 hour, "Babylonian Local Time" is

$$t_{\text{Bab}} = t_{\text{Grw}} + 3^{\text{h}}.$$

In this edition, the modern computations have been designated by Universal Time (UT), which, as stated before, is the equivalent of Greenwich Mean Time. The equivalence in UT for Babylonian Local Time is then

$$t_{\text{Bab}} = \text{UT} + 3^{\text{h}}.$$

---

[8] In *Diaries* Vol.I, p.15.

[9] B. Tuckerman, *Planetary, Lunar, and Solar Positions: 601 B.C. to A.D. 1.* (American Philosophical Society, Philadelphia, 1962, reprint 1990).

[10] H.Hunger-R. Dvorak, *Ephemeriden von Sonne, Mond und hellen Planeten von -1000 bis -601.* (Verlag der Österreichischen Akademie der Wissenschaften, Vienna, 1981).

Since the time designations in the texts are generally with respect to some division of the day of several hours duration (e.g., "last part of night," or "first watch"[11]), rarely specified to within an hour, the moments chosen for modern computation of longitudes reflect only approximations. If the horoscope indicates that the birth occurred e.g., "before morning" (*ina* ZALÁG), the time of sunrise can be determined and then some approximation of a moment before that be estimated as the time of birth. For example, in the case of Text 20, dated -125 Aug.16, it was determined that sunrise occurred at 2.40 UT. Relative to this time, 2 UT was chosen as a basis for computing longitudes.

In my note to each table of astronomical data following the editions of each horoscope, I have anachronistically translated the approximated Babylonian time of birth to a time of day in accordance with the midnight epoch. Therefore, as in the example just mentioned (Text 20), if the birth time is estimated as occurring at or around 2 UT, in accordance with the above equivalence $t_{Bab} = UT + 3^h$, I have stated the "Babylonian Local Time" as 5 AM. This has been added as a convenient translation not only of the temporal designations as they appear (or must be reconstructed) in the texts, i.e., the native Babylonian terms, but also of the time references devised for use in astronomical chronology (such as Universal Time).

§ 3 TEXT INDICES

§ 3.1 *Catalogue of Horoscopes and Birth Notes*

Horoscopes

Text No.	*Museum No.*	*Year Date*
1	AO 17649	-409
2	AB 251	-409
3	BM 32376	-297
4	BM 33382	-287
5	MLC 1870	-262
6a	BM 47721	-258
6b	BM 47721	-250
7	BM 33667	-257
8	BM 36943	-250
9	NCBT 1231	-248
10	MLC 2190	-234
11	W 20030/143	-234
12	BM 33741	-229

---

[11] See chapter 3§ 2.3.

13	BM 47642	-223
14	BM 36620	-219
15	BM 36796	-201
16a	W 20030/10	-199
16b	W 20030/10	-198
17	BM 41054	-175
18	BM 35516	-141
19	BM 81561	-139
20	BM 78089	-125
21	BM 33018	-124
22a	BM 41301	-116
22b	BM 41301	-114
23	BM 34003	-87
24	BM 77265	-82
25	BM 42025	-80
26	BM 35515	-75
27	BM 38104	-68
28	BM 37374	?

Birth Notes

29	BM 64148	-368
30	BM 33563	-292
31	BM 34693	-213
32	BM 34567	-114, -116, -153

§ *3.2 Index to Edited Texts*

Provenance is Babylon unless otherwise indicated.

Mus.Number	Previous pub.	Date	Comments	Text No.
AB 251	Thompson, CLBT 2;			
	JCS 6 54-57	-409	Babylon(?)	2
AO 17649	Arnaud TBER 6 52	Darius 13 -409	Nippur	1
BM 32376	unpub.	S.E. 13 -297		3
BM 33018	L*1468; Centaurus 32	S.E. 187 -124		21
BM 33382	L*1459	S.E. 24 -287		4
BM 33563	=RmIV 119	S.E. 19 -292	birth note	30
BM 33667	JCS 6 58-60	S.E. 54 -257		7
BM 33741	JCS 6 61-62	S.E. 82 -229		12
BM 34003	L 1470	S.E. 223 -88		23

BM 34567	L**1469; JCS 6 65	S.E. 197 -114	birth note	32
BM 34693	L*1465	S.E. 98 -213	birth note	31
BM 35515	L*1474	S.E. 236 -75		26
BM 35516	JCS 6 62-63	S.E. 169 -141		18
BM 36620	L*1464	S.E. 92 -219		14
BM 36796	L*1466	S.E. 109 -202		15
BM 36943	unpub.	S.E. 61 -250		8
BM 37374	unpub.	?		28
BM 38104	L*1475	S.E. 243 -68		27
BM 41054	unpub.	S.E. 135 -175		17
BM 41301	unpub.	S.E. 195 -116	two horoscopes	22a
		S.E. 197 -114		22b
BM 42025+	L*1472f.	S.E. 231 -80	joins 42164	25
BM 42164	L 1473		see 42025+	
BM 47642	unpub.	S.E. 88 -223		13
BM 47721	unpub.	S.E.[ ] -258	two horoscopes	6a
		S.E. 61 -250		6b
BM 64148	unpub.	Artax.II 36 -368	birth note	29
BM 77265	L*1471	S.E. 229 -82		24
BM 78089	unpub.	S.E. 186 -125		20
BM 81561	unpub.	S.E. 172 -139		19
MLC 1870	JCS 6 57-58	S.E. 48 -262	Uruk	5
MLC 2190	JCS 6 60-61	S.E. 77 -234	Uruk	10
NCBT 1231	unpub.	S.E. 63 -248	Uruk	9
W 20030/10	BagM.Bei 2 81	S.E. 112 -199	Uruk; two horoscopes	16a
		S.E. 113 -198		16b
W 20030/143	BagM.Beih. 2 82	S.E. 77 -234	Uruk; dupl. MLC 2190	11

CHAPTER 3:
Elements of a Babyonian Horoscope

§ 1 BASIC TERMINOLOGY

§ 1.1 *The Names of the Planets*

The horoscopes use the abbreviated names of the planets familiar from non-mathematical astronomical texts and mathematical ephemerides. The forms as they appear in earlier corpora, such as celestial omens (the series *Enūma Anu Enlil*) and MUL.APIN, are retained only in the occasional use of the writing ^dUTU (*Šamaš*) for the sun, and in the name for Venus (*Delebat*), which, unlike the logogram ^dUTU, persists in all late astronomical texts. The following shows the names as they appear in horoscope texts as against omens (whose conventions are consistent with MUL.APIN) and mathematical astronomical texts.[1]

	Akkadian	HOROSCOPES	OMENS and MUL.APIN	ACT
Moon	*Sin*	30	^d30, ^dEN.ZU, DINGIR	30
Sun	*Šamaš*	20, ^dUTU	^d20, ^dUTU	20
Jupiter	?[2]	MÚL.BABBAR	SAG.ME.GAR, PA.ME.GAR	BABBAR
Venus	*Delebat*	*Dele-bat*	^d*Dele-bat*, ^d15	*Dele-bat*
Mercury	*Šiḫṭu*	GU₄.UD	^dUDU.IDIM.GU₄.UD	GU₄
Saturn	*Kajamānu*	GENNA	^dUDU.IDIM.SAG.UŠ	GENNA
Mars	*Salbatānu*	AN	^d*Sal-bat-a-nu*	AN

Note that in the text transcriptions, the practice of Sachs to transcribe 30 as *sin* and 20 as *šamáš* is followed.

§ 1.2 *The Names of the Zodiacal Signs*

The zodiacal signs (*lumāšu* =LU.MAŠ.MEŠ), consisting of twelve 30-degree segments of the ecliptic, came about as a result of the stan-

---

[1] For discussion of the knowledge of Babylonian planet names in Greco-Roman tradition, see F. Cumont, "Les noms des planetes et l'astrolatrie chez les Grecs," *L'Antiquite Classique* 4 (1935), pp.5-43, and R.R. Stieglitz, "The Chaldeo-Babylonian Planet Names in Hesychius," Y.L. Arbeitman ed., *Fucus: A Semitic/Afrasian gathering in remembrance of Albert Ehrman* (= *Current Issues in Linguistic Theory* 58, 1988), pp.443-447.

[2] The Akkadian reading of the name SAG.ME.GAR is uncertain. Other names for the planet Jupiter, such as ^dŠUL.PA.È.A, UD.AL.TAR (*Dāpinu*), and *Nēberu*, are encountered in omen texts, reports, and MUL.APIN, but whose equivalent is not found in horoscope texts, which refer to the planet only by the name MÚL.BABBAR "The White Star," consistent with Seleucid usage.

dardization of twelve ecliptical constellations through which the sun could be seen to travel in one ideal "year" of twelve 30-day months. Ecliptical constellations, defined as stars "in the path of the moon (*ḫarrān Sin*)," were identified at least by the second quarter of the first millennium B.C. A list enumerating the stars in the path of the moon is included in MUL.APIN I iv 31-39. The names of the zodiacal signs derive from an original relation to the ecliptical constellations. Once the signs were defined by degrees of longitude, normed by fixed stars, rather than by the actual boundaries of the constellation, however, they ceased to have any real relation to the constellations and became an astronomical reference system, which was simultaneously a numerical system effective for computing ecliptical positions. Our evidence places this development sometime during the fifth century B.C.

The following table gives the names of the signs of the zodiac as they appear in the horoscopes. Since the extant horoscopes come primarily from the Seleucid period, the terminology is essentially the same as that of the mathematical astronomical texts and other late Babylonian astro-nomical texts. Some of the abbreviated forms of the zodiacal sign names, such as MAŠ for MAŠ.MAŠ "Gemini,"[3] and MÚL for MÚL.MÚL "Taurus,"[4] typically found in ACT, occur in one of the Uruk horoscopes, while others, such as GÍR for GÍR.TAB "Scorpius," and ZIB for ZIB.ME "Pisces," do not appear in any of the horoscope texts. A number of older spellings not attested in ACT, such as GU$_4$.AN "Taurus," and UR.A "Leo," are still found in the horoscopes.

Zodiacal Sign	*Horoscopes*
Aries	HUN, LU (for LÚ from ^{LÚ}HUN.GÁ) "The Hireling"
Taurus	GU$_4$.AN "Bull of Heaven", MÚL.MÚL "The Stars"
Gemini	MAŠ.MAŠ "The Great Twins"
Cancer	ALLA "The Crab"
Leo	A, UR.A "The Lion"
Virgo	ABSIN "The Furrow"
Libra	RÍN "The Scales"
Scorpius	GÍR.TAB "The Scorpion"
Sagittarius	PA
Capricorn	MÁŠ "The Goat-fish"
Aquarius	GU "The Great One"
Pisces	KUN, KUN.MEŠ, ZIB.ME "The Tails"

---

[3] Text 16 rev. 5.

[4] Text 16:3 and rev.8.

The earliest cuneiform evidence for the existence of the zodiac comes from fifth century astronomical diary texts (e.g. No. -453 iv 2 and upper edge 2-3, No.-440 rev.3', and No.-418:5, 10, rev.8' and 14')[5] and horoscopes (Texts 1 and 2, both dated -409), in which positions of the planets are cited with respect to zodiacal signs. The existence of the zodiac in this period is also indirectly supported by Seleucid astronomical texts that deal with phenomena of the Achaemenid period. The oldest of these relates longitudes of conjunctions of the sun and moon, computed by a schematic method, with solar eclipses. The phenomena computed in these texts can be dated with relative certainty to -474, although the writing of the tablets was certainly much later.[6] Another text that uses the zodiac together with astronomical phenomena dated to ca. -430[7] lists phenomena for Venus and Mars plus a column containing values of "col.Φ" in the Babylonian lunar theory.[8]

Diagnostic of the use of zodiacal signs, as opposed to constellations, is the terminology *ina* "in," *ina* SAG "at the beginning of," or *ina* TIL "at the end," of a sign. In the very early diary texts the terminology seems not to be fully differentiated, so that a simple *ina* starname may refer to a zodiacal constellation rather than a sign.[9] In Seleucid period texts, such as the horoscopes (except Texts 1 and 2), the terminology "at the beginning/ the end" followed by a starname always refers to a zodiacal sign. Texts 12:3, 17:5, and 20:4 contain lunar positions "at the beginning of" (*ina* SAG) a zodiacal sign, and text 15:5 has "at the end of" (*ina* TIL) followed by the zodiacal sign. Texts 5:5 and 9:5 contain positions of Jupiter "at the beginning" of a zodiacal sign.

§ 1.3 *The Names of Fixed Stars*

Omens based upon the appearances of fixed stars are known from

---

[5] Sachs-Hunger, *Diaries* Vol.I. The references in diary No.-463:3', 7', and 12' are not yet clearly distinguishable from zodiacal constellations, although could already be zodiacal signs. Note also the lunar text LBAT 1427 obv. 11'-12', in which the writing of the sign Taurus, GU₄.AN, is found for an eclipse of -407: 1 KÙŠ *ina* IGI GU₄.AN GÍR "1 cubit in front of Taurus (the moon) was eclipsed." In the same text, obv. 6' a reference to Sagittarius is found in an eclipse report from -408: ina KI PA GÍR "in the region of Sagittarius (the moon) was eclipsed."

[6] A.Aaboe and A. Sachs, "Two Lunar Texts of the Achaemenid Period from Babylon," *Centaurus* 14 (1969), p.17, Text B obv. col.v with heading *lu-maš* "zodiacal sign."

[7] O.Neugebauer and A.Sachs, "Some Atypical Astronomical Cuneiform Texts. I," JCS 21 (1967), p.193, 197-8, Text C.

[8] See discussion in J.P. Britton, "An Early Function for Eclipse Magnitudes in Babylonian Astronomy," *Centaurus* 32 (1989), pp.1-52.

[9] See Sachs-Hunger *Diaries* No.-453 up.edge 2.

Enūma Anu Enlil,[10] but no mention is made of fixed star phases in the horoscopes. The references to stars in horoscopes are confined to the use of the ecliptical stars as a set of observational reference points. The Babylonian term for these stars was *kakkabū minâti* (MUL.ŠID.MEŠ) "counting stars," but have come to be known in modern terminology as normal stars after Epping's term *Normalsterne*.[11] These stars lie close to the ecliptic, i.e., falling within a fairly narrow band of latitude between +10° and -7;30° within which the moon and planets can be seen. The normal stars are most commonly found in the non-mathematical astronomical texts, especially the diaries, and normal star almanacs derived from the diaries. No complete list as such is attested in an ancient source, but about 34 normal stars are presently known. A useful list of the 32 most commonly occurring may be found in Sachs-Hunger, *Diaries*, pp.17-19.

The normal stars provided a positional system in which distance with respect to a certain normal star was noted in cubits (KÙŠ= *ammatu*) and fingers (ŠU.SI= *ubānu*) where 24 fingers equal 1 cubit, and 12 fingers equal 1 degree.[12] Directional terms "above" and "below" normal stars are more difficult to interpret.[13] The normal stars as an ecliptical reference system are utilized in the horoscopes exclusively for citing the position of the moon.[14] In these few horoscopes, the position of the moon seems to be given with reference to a normal star when it is above the horizon at (or near) the time of the birth, and usually is given in addition to a zodiacal position. The normal star positions found in the horoscopes are almost certainly extracted from astronomical diaries.

Only nine fixed stars are found mentioned in the extant horoscopes. Excepting Texts 4 and 7, the horoscopes which quote normal star positions for the moon also give a zodiacal position following the statement of the time of birth. The following lists the normal stars with their standard names in order of their position in the ecliptic, with the textual references

---

[10] Eg., Reiner-Pingree, BPO 2, pp.56-59 (Text IX).

[11] Epping, *Astronomisches aus Babylon* (Freiburg, 1889), p.115; Kugler, SSB I Tafel XXIV, and SSB II pp.550-553. For MUL.ŠID.MEŠ, see Sachs-Hunger, *Diaries*, No. -136, and O. Neugebauer and A.Sachs, "Some Atypical Astronomical Cuneiform Texts, " JCS 21 (1967), p.201, Text E rev. 1, 5, 10, 13, 16, 18, and 21.

[12] O. Neugebauer, ACT I, p.39; O.Neugebauer and A. Sachs, "Some Atypical Astronomical Cuneiform Texts I," (1967), pp.204- 205; O. Neugebauer, HAMA p.591; M. Powell, RlA s.v. "Masse." G. Grasshoff pointed out in a paper read at the Dibner Institute-MIT conference on Babylonian and Greek astronomy, May 6-8, 1994, that the 24-fingers/cubit is not consistent with the evidence, and that fingers may not be in any fixed relation to the cubit. Proceedings of this conference are forthcoming, edited by Noel Swerdlow (1998).

[13] HAMA p.546.

[14] Texts 2, 4, 6, 7, 8, 13, 14, 15, and 17.

to where they occur. Longitudes are computed in the commentary to the texts. Note the variation allowable in the forms of the star names.

1) MÚL KUR *šá* DUR *nu-nu* = η Piscium
    30 SIG *nūnu* moon below (the Bright Star of the Ribbon of the) Fishes Text 7
    rev. 2
    [SIG?] MÚL KUR *šá* DU[R *nūnu*] (moon) [below] the Bright Star of the Ribb[on of the Fishes] Text 8:2

2) MÚL IGI *šá* SAG HUN = β Arietis
    30 SIG MÚL IGI *šá* SAG HUN moon below the Front Star of the Head of the Hired Man   Text 7:2

3) MÚL *ár* *šá* SAG HUN   = α Arietis
    [30] SIG MÚL *ár* *šá* SAG HUN   moon below the Rear Star of the Head of the Hired Man Text 14:3

4) ŠUR GIGIR *šá* SI = β Tauri
    30 *ina* IGI ŠUR *šá* SI moon west of the Northern ... of the Chariot Text 15:3

5) ŠUR GIGIR *šá* ULÙ = ζ Tauri
    30 *ina* IGI ŠUR GIGIR *šá* ULÙ moon west of the "Southern ... of the Chariot," Text 4:3
    30 *ina* IGI ŠUR ULÙ moon west of the Southern ... (of the Chariot) Text 15:3

6) SAG A   = ε Leonis
    30 *ina* SAG A moon in the Head of the Lion   Text 21:4 The formulation *ina* "in" + Starname, however, argues for an   interpretation of A here as the zodiacal sign Leo and SAG as the construct *rēš* "beginning of." See Text 21 commentary.

7) DELE *šá* IGI ABSIN = γ Virginis
    30 *ár* DELE *šá* IGI AB[SIN] moon behind the Single star in front of the Fur[row] Text 6 rev.2

8) SA₄ *šá* ABSIN = α Virginis
    30 SIG SA₄ *šá* ABSIN moon below the Bright Star of the Furrow Text 13:3

9) SI GÍR.TAB
    30 *šap-lat* SI GÍR.TAB moon below "Pincer of the Scorpion" Text

> 2:3; not one of the recognized Normal Stars (see discussion of
> Sachs, JCS 6 p.55), but in the vicinity of α and β Librae.

For the longitudes of these normal stars cited in horoscope texts, I have
interpolated from the list giving ecliptic coordinates for the years -600, -300,
and 0, available in Sachs-Hunger, *Diaries* I pp.17-19.

§ 2 CALENDARIC DATA

The Babylonian horoscopes were all dated to the birth of a child. Three
texts contain more than one horoscope (Texts 6, 16, and 22), and so clearly
in these cases the horoscopes were collected *ex post facto*. The evidence that
data were excerpted from other astronomical texts, such as diaries,
almanacs, and even goal-year texts, indicates that a horoscope represents
some compilation of observations taken from other documents, or indeed
computations of heavenly phenomena, put together sometime after the
date of birth. Given the existence of the birthnotes, which preserve dates
and times of births, it is clear that horoscopes could have been prepared
any time after such dates. In the single birthnote preserved with more than
one date (Text 32), two of the dates are spaced 36 years. In no case has a
horoscope tablet been dated or signed by the scribe by means of a
colophon. The dates given are invariably at the beginning of the text and
refer exclusively to the birth date.

§ 2. 1. Years and Eras

The dating of the births is by regnal year before the Seleucid Era, and
then by Seleucid Era year number thereafter. After the institution of the
Seleucid Era, in which regnal years were no longer of consequence for the
calendar, the name of the king was still sometimes identified, as in the
examples listed below. Following the Parthian institution of the Arsacid
Era, occasionally both S.E. and A.E. year numbers were given (for the only
example among horoscopes, see Text 20).

The following are attested Achaemenid regnal years:

MU.13 ¹*Dar-ia-a-muš* = -409 Darius II (Text 1)
MU.36 ¹*Ar-tak-šat-su* = -368 Artaxerxes II (Text 29, a birth note)

Seleucid Era years, identifying king, or coregencies:
MU.19.KAM ¹Se-lu-uk LUGAL = -292 Seleucus I Nicator (Text 30, a
    birth note)
MU.24.KAM ¹*Se u* ¹*An* LUGAL.MEŠ = -287 Seleucus I and Antiochus I
    Soter (Text 4)
MU.KU.1 ¹*An-ti-'u-uk-su* LUGAL = -250 Antiochus II Theos (Text 6)
[MU].⌈1⌉,28.KAM ¹*Se-lu-ku* LUGAL = -223 Seleucus III Soter (Text 13)

MU.1,32.K[AM ^1An LUGAL] = -219 Antiochus III "The Great" (Text 14)
MU.1,49!.KAM ^{1} *An u* ^{1} *An* A-*šú* LUGAL.MEŠ = -201 Antiochus III
and Antiochus (Text 15)
[MU.1,]⸢36⸣.KAM ^{1}*Se-lu-ku* LUGAL =-175 Seleucus IV Philopator (Text
    17)
[MU.1.M]E.1,9.KAM ^{1}*Di-mit-ri* [LUGAL] =-141 Demetrios II Nicator
    (Text 18)[15]

Parthian period year dates:
    Following the installation in 141 B.C. of the Arsacid Parthians, names
of regents are not given in the horoscopes, only the dynastic name
"Arsaces." This is the practice in other cuneiform texts of the period,
which makes the identification of the individual regents somewhat
difficult.[16] Note that the first horoscope dated to the Parthian period (Text
19) comes from the first year after the institution of double-dating by
Seleucid and Arsacid eras. When only one year number is given, it is the
Seleucid era number, with indication that the king was Arsacid (as in Text
21).
    MU.1.ME 1,12.KAM ^{1}*Ar-šá-ka-a* LUGAL = -139 Arsaces, was Mithradates
        I (Text 19)
    ⸢MU.1.ME.22.KAM *ša ší* MU.1.ME.1,26.KAM⸣ ^{1}*Ar-šá-ka-a* LUGAL = -125
        (year 122 A.E. which is 186 S.E.) Arsaces, was Artabanus II (Text
        20)
    MU.1.ME.1,27.KAM ^{1}*Ar-šá-kam* LUGAL = -124 Arsaces, was Artabanus
        II (Text 21)
    [MU.1.ME.1,35.KAM ^{1}]*Ar-[šá-kam* LUGAL] = -116 Arsaces, was   Mithra-
        dates II "The Great" (Text 22 a)
    [MU.1.ME.1,3]7.KAM ^{1}⸢*Ar*⸣ LUGAL = -114 Arsaces, was Mithradates II
        "The Great" (Text 22 b)
    MU.2.ME.23.KA[M ^{1}*Ar-šá-kam* LUGAL] = -87 Arsaces, was Gotarzes I
        (Text 23)
    [MU.2.ME.29 ^{1}*Ar-šá-kam* LUGAL] =-82 Arsaces, was Gotarzes I (Text 24)[17]
    MU.2.ME.36.KAM ^{1}*Ar-šá-kam* LUGAL = -75, was Orodes I (Text 26)[18]

---

[15] This represents the year before the Parthians under Mithradates I (ca. 171-139/8 B.C.)
took control of Seleucia on the Tigris. See N. Debevoise, *A Political History of Parthia*
(Chicago, 1938).

[16] See J. Oelsner, *Materialien zur babylonischen Gesellschaft und Kultur in hellenistischer
Zeit* (Budapest, 1986), p.275 note r.

[17] On the uncertainties of rule in this year, see N. Debevoise, *A Political History of Parthia*
(Chicago, 1938), pp.48-52 and Richard N. Frye, *The History of Ancient Iran* (Munich,
1984), pp.214-15. See also J. Oelsner, *Materialien zur babylonischen Gesellschaft und Kultur
in hellenistischer Zeit* (Budapest, 1986), pp.276-7.

[18] According to Parker-Dubberstein, p.24 and Brinkman's "Mesopotamian Chronology,"

§ 2.2 Months

As in the diaries, some horoscopes indicate the first day of the month of the birth by means of 30 or 1. In a luni-solar calendar with uses true lunar months of 29;31,50,7 (29.5309) days duration, no months have an integer number of days. Because of the fraction of a day over 29, a lunar month is experienced as either 29 or 30 days. The Babylonian convention of writing 30 following the month name meant that day 1 fell on the "30th" day of the preceding month. This succinctly indicated that the preceding month was hollow, or had 29 days. The number 1 following the month name indicated that the previous month had 30 days, or was full.

The month names are those of the standard Babylonian calendar, written with the logograms used in omen literature as well as astronomical texts:

BARA$_2$ = *Nisannu* (March/April)
GU$_4$ = *Ajaru* (April/May)
SIG = *Simanu* (May/June)
ŠU = *Du'ūzu* (June/July)
NE = *Abu* (July/August)
KIN = *Ulūlu* August/September)
DU$_6$ = *Tašrītu* (September/October)
APIN = *Arahsamna* (October/November)
GAN = *Kislīmu* (November/December)
AB = *Ṭebētu* (December/January)
ZÍZ = *Šabaṭu* (January/February)
ŠE = *Addaru* (February/March)
ŠE.DIRI = *Addaru arkû*   intercalary Addaru

Note that the intercalary sixth month *Ulūlu arkû* , which is found in the late Babylonian astronomical texts, is not used, or at least is not attested, in the horoscopes.

§ 2.3. Time of day and night

Expressions for the divisions of the day attested in the horoscopes and birthnotes may be roughly classified into three systems of dividing time: (a) a three-part division of the night into watches, (b) a four-part division of the nychthemeron with respect to sunrise and sunset, and (c) a twelve-part division of the day-time into hours, whose length varied with the season.

§   2.3.1 The tripartite division of the night was in the following "watches"

in Oppenheim, *Ancient Mesopotamia*, p.342, the date of this text corresponds to the last year of the reign of Orodes I. See also Oelsner, *Materialien*, p.277, and Debevoise, *A Political History of Parthia*, pp.52-53.

(*maṣṣarātu*): EN.NUN AN.USÁN *barārītu* evening watch, EN.NUN MURUB₄ *qablītu* middle watch, and EN.NUN U₄.ZAL.LA *šāt urri* morning watch, with variant, EN.NUN ZALÁG.GA *namārītu* watch of dawn. The watches of the night comprise the earliest system of "telling time" attested in Babylonian texts, being used in celestial omens as well as non-scientific contexts already in the Old Babylonian period.[19] In horoscopes the watches are used in the following expressions:

> USÁN   evening watch (Text 15, and 19)
> MURUB₄ GE₆ middle of night (Text 23)
> *mišil* GE₆ middle of night (Text 24)
> *ina* MURUB₄-*tim* in the middle watch (of night) (Text 31:8)

Another common expression, but distinct from the use of the evening watch to denote early night, is SAG GE₆ "beginning of night." The astronomical diaries also distinguish between evening watch (USÁN) and the expression SAG GE₆, although the duration of the latter is difficult to determine from its use in context.[20] SAG GE₆ is found in the following horoscopes:

Text 6 rev. 2 [ITI.G]U₄ 30 GE₆ 8 SAG GE₆ (moon in advance of β/ζ Tauri) "[Aj]aru 30, night of the 8th, beginning of night," followed by the normal star position of the moon. This time designation, therefore, is not used with respect to the birth, which is given in line 3 as one-half *bēru* before sunset. Line 2 appears to be a quote from a diary giving the lunar position with respect to a normal star on the 8th day. Hunger has pointed out that the term SAG GE₆ seems to correlate with the lunar data given for the first half of the month.[21] Indeed, after day 10 or so, once the moon is past quadrature and it sets at midnight, SAG GE₆ is not used.

Text 13:2 [IT]I.NE 30 GE₆ 4 SAG GE ₆ (moon below α Virginis) "[Ab]u 30, night of the 4th, beginning of night," followed by the normal star position of the moon. This is parallel to the passage in Text 6, and appears to be a line quoted from a diary. Again the birth occurs in the first half of the month.

Text 15:2 is consistent with the horoscopes just mentioned. The birth day was the ninth of the month. The lunar datum quoted from a diary therefore refers to the first half of the month. The horoscope gives the time of birth not as the beginning of night, but as the evening watch. Similarly, some diaries will use both these designations, citing SAG GE₆ before

---

[19] In CAD sub *maṣṣartu* 3d, and in celestial omens, the watches are attested in Old Babylonian eclipse omens, e.g., BM 22696 obv. 1 (*barartim*), 2 (MURUB₄, var. *qablītim*) and 3 (*šāt urri*).

[20] See Sachs-Hunger, Diaries Vol.I p.15.

[21] Sachs-Hunger, Diaries Vol. I p.15.

USÁN, if both are used.

In Text 18:2-4, the birthdate is the sixth of the month. Again, the normal star position of the moon is taken directly from a diary, hence the use of SAG GE$_6$ in association with a date before quadrature. The time of the birth in this horoscope, however, is in the last part of the night (*ina* ZALÁG). Obviously, the moon was no longer above the horizon at the time of birth, just before sunrise. A (computed) zodiacal lunar position is also given, as is customary in the horoscopes which quote normal star positions for the moon.

§ 2.3.2 The four parts of the day, defined with respect to sunset and sunrise are: GE$_6$ GIN "after sunset" (between sunset and midnight), GE$_6$ *ana* ZALAG$_2$ "before sunrise" (between midnight and sunrise), ME NIM "after sunrise" (between sunrise and noon), and *ana* ŠÚ *šamáš* "before sunset"(between noon and sunset). The following are found in horoscopes:

> GE$_6$ *ana* ZALÁG (so many UŠ of) night until sunrise/morning (Text 32:6)
> ME *ana* ŠÚ *šamáš* (so many UŠ of) daylight until sunset (Text 6b rev.3).

These expressions, and their variations,[22] are found in late Babylonian non-mathematical astronomical texts, as well as in procedures, such as ACT procedure text 200 obv. ii 21, rev. ii 16, from Babylon. The designation of the amount of night before daybreak GE$_6$ *ana* ZALÁG in non-mathematical astronomical texts is also and equivalently expressed with the term KUR, itself an abbreviation of KUR (or, *ana* KUR) *Šamáš*, literally "before sunrise."

Two other expressions are attested, which are not identical to any found in the non-mathematical astronomical texts, but seem to refer to the same system of dividing the day: The first is *ina* ZALÁG "in the last part of night/ morning" (Texts 1, 18, 20), which recalls the term GE$_6$ *ana* ZALÁG, mentioned above. The other is *panat* KUR 20 before sunrise, which seems to refer to the same time division as does *ina* ZALÁG. The word ZALÁG, which in the expression *ina namāri* "at dawn" comes from *namāru* "to dawn (as of the day)," and is synonymous with *šêru* "to become morning" (Malku VI 212).[23] should be taken as the technical designation for dawn, specifically, the interval from daybreak to sunrise.[24]

§ 2.3.3. The division of the day (and night) into twelve equal portions from sunrise to sunset (and sunset to sunrise) regardless of season, so that

---

[22] See "Excursus I: The Epochs of the Day," in Neugebauer and Sachs, "Atypical Astronomical Cuneiform Texts," JCS 21 (1967), p.212-213.

[23] See CAD s.v. *namāru* lexical section.

[24] The specific sense of "dawn" used here follows that suggested by B. R. Goldstein in his review of G. Toomer's *Ptolemy's Almagest*, see *Isis* 76 (1985), p.117.

the hour itself increases and decreases its length through the year is known as the seasonal hour. The Akkadian term found for this time unit is *simānu* "hour."[25] The system of time reckoning by seasonal hour, according to which the daytime and night each were divided into twelve equal portions is first attested in the seventh century, in material such as a Neo-Babylonian arithmetical scheme for the variation in the length of the subdivisions of the day (the values given represented one-twelfth of the length of daylight)[26] and, later, in horoscopes. [27] In Greek astronomy, seasonal hours make their debut with an early third century B.C. observational report of Timocharis, preserved in the *Almagest*.[28] The following is the formula used in the Babylonian horoscopes :

> *ina* n^{th} *siman* in the nth hour (of the day/night).

With the use of seasonal hours it seems the distinction between day hour or night was indicated by the use of either U_4 or GE_6 when giving the day number, e.g., Text 21:3 U_4.22 ina 11 *siman šerru alid* "the child was born on the 22nd day in the 11th hour (in the daytime)." This formula is preserved also in Texts 22, 26, and 27. The term alone is preserved in broken context in half the extant horoscopes.

§ 2.3.4. Units of time

As discussed in section 3 above, the time designations in the horoscopes are given with respect to the larger divisions of the day. Expressions with the standard units of time measurement, the UŠ "time degree" (= 4 minutes of time) and the DANNA (*bēru*) "double hour" (= 30 UŠ or 120 minutes) are rarely encountered. It is presumed here that the use of *bēru* in these texts reflects the same seasonally unvarying division of time as does the use of UŠ, i.e., one *bēru* is equal to 30 UŠ.[29] Two examples are found in the context of the measured duration of the lunar NA:

> Text 2:7 BAR 1 28 14(?) 4,40(?) "Nisannu 1, 28 (UŠ, the duration of lunar visibility after sunset), on the 14th day, 4,40 (UŠ, the duration of lunar visibility

---

[25] See my, "Babylonian Seasonal Hours," *Centaurus* 32 (1989), pp.146-170.

[26] E. Reiner and D. Pingree, "A Neo-Babylonian Report on Seasonal Hours," *Archiv für Orientforschung* 25 (1977), pp.50-55.

[27] See my "Babylonian Seasonal Hours," *Centaurus* 32 (1989), pp.146-170.

[28] See B.R. Goldstein and A.C. Bowen, "On Early Hellenistic Astronomy Timocharis and the First Callippic Calendar," *Centaurus* 32 (1989), pp.272-293, especially pp.274-276. The date of the report in question is -294.

[29] See F.R. Stephenson and L.J. Fatoohi, "The Babylonian Unit of Time," *JHA* 25 (1994), pp.99-110.

after sunrise)."

Text 7 r.5 13 11 NA *ša* ^{d}*Sin* "The 13th day, 11 (UŠ was the duration of) lunar visibility after sunrise."

And two more examples are found in the context of the designation of the native's time of birth, given with respect to the divisions of day and night by sunrise and sunset (see above sub 3b):

Text 6 r.3 U₄ 8 *ša* 30 DANNA ME *ana* ⌜ŠÚ⌝ *šamáš a-lid* "The 8th day, at one-half *bēru* (= 15 UŠ = 1 hour) before sunset (the native) was born."

Text 32:5-6 ZÍZ GE₆ 10 30 DANNA GE₆ *ana* ZALÁG LÚ.TUR *a-lid* "Month XI night of the 10th, one-half *bēru* (= 1 hour) remaining until sunrise, the native was born."

§ 3. ASTRONOMICAL DATA

The goal of the Babylonian horoscopes was to collect certain astronomical data for a particular date, and in some cases, for a particular time of night or day. The kinds of celestial phenomena collected in the horoscope texts are briefly outlined in this section, but details will be found in the commentaries to individual texts.

§ 3.1. Lunar
§ 3.1.1. Position in the Ecliptic

This is established either with respect to a normal star, quoted from an astronomical diary (see above sub 1.3), or by the zodiac. The moon's longitude with respect to a zodiacal sign is always given, even if a normal star position has already been cited. Less often, a zodiacal longitude is given in degrees within a sign.

§ 3.1.2. Lunar Three Data

The length of the previous month is indicated by 30 or 1, the date of mid-month NA,[30] the time between sunrise and moonset, and the date of KUR, or day of last lunar crescent are given. This terminology is standard in late Babylonian astronomical texts. Exceptionally, the older term U₄.NÁ.ÀM (*bubbulu*) "day of last visibility" occurs in one text (Text 2:8).[31] It appears from the regular inclusion of these dates that the moon's position at the syzygies during the month of the birth was astrologically importan'
Although the distribution of preserved diaries does not provide any overlap
for the lunar three data in horoscopes, it is almost a certainty that these

---

[30] Note the less abbreviated NA *ša* ^{d}*Sin* in Text 7 r.5.

[31] Note the use of U₄.NÁ.ÀM as well in ACT 200 r.ii 15, a procedure text for computing the day of last visibility of the moon.

data represent extracts from diaries in the same way as do the normal star references to the position of the moon.

Omens for the dates of first visibility and full moon are well known from *Enūma Anu Enlil* and the attention to these dates is also abundantly attested to in the Neo-Assyrian reports. A late Uruk celestial omen text combines these dates so that the protasis states, for example *šumma* UD.30.KAM *innamirma unnut* UD.13.KAM *lu* UD.14.KAM *izziz mahīru imatti* "if (the moon) becomes visible on the 30th day and is dim, and stands in opposition (with the sun) on the 13th or the 14th day: the market will decrease."[32] The positive or negative portent of syzygy dates could figure in the interpretation of a personal horoscope, but this is sheer speculation. At any rate, corresponding zodiacal positions of the moon on the dates of NA and KUR are not provided in the horoscope texts. The dates of the syzygies, however, appear to be essential data for all the horoscopes from Babylon, taking into consideration broken passages. The tradition from Uruk appears to be different. None of the Uruk horoscopes include the lunar three, despite their giving a position of the moon in the ecliptic.

§ 3.1.3. Lunar Eclipses

In the Babylonian astronomical literature, a distinction between computed and observed lunar eclipses is conveyed in the writing of "lunar eclipse," as AN.KU$_{10}$ *sin* when computed and *sin* AN.KU$_{10}$ when observed.[33] This practice can be seen in the non-mathematical astronomical literature, where context clearly determines whether one is in the presence of observations or computations. For example, the almanacs and normal star almanacs give computed eclipses, whereas observational eclipse reports are found in diaries and their derivative texts. Since the eclipses recorded in the horoscopes are exclusively expressed with AN.KU$_{10}$ *sin*, they should not be regarded as observed. Further support for this interpretation is the feature, present in all the preserved eclipse passages, of citing the zodiacal sign in which the eclipse occurred, or, specifically, in which totality occurred. For example, the third century horoscope Text 4 rev.3-4 has: "Arahsamna the 13th, a lunar eclipse occurred, totality (occurred) in Taurus." The second century Text 22a rev.8' has: "Ulūlu the 14th, a lunar eclipse occurred, totality (occurred) in Aries." The presence of the zodiacal sign unequivocally indicates some form of computation. However, given the compiled nature of these documents, it seems unlikely that direct computations were used for the eclipses cited in horoscopes.

As shown in Table 3.1 below, the eclipses cited in horoscopes occurred on dates quite removed from that of the date of birth. In view of this, it is

---

[32] Hunger Uruk I 94: 18.

[33] See Sachs-Hunger, Diaries I, p.23.

clear that extracting astronomical data from a diary text paragraph corresponding to the month and day of the birth would not have been sufficient.

When one considers the content of the *Enūma Anu Enlil* lunar eclipse omens, a great many aspects of eclipses appear to have become astrologically significant at a relatively early date, since the series as a whole was formed by the Neo-Assyrian period. In the protases of these omens are included the elements of the date of occurrence (month, day), the time (watch of night), the magnitude (in fingers), direction of eclipse shadow, and color of the eclipse.[34] The lunar eclipses cited in horoscopes are there presumably for what they contribute to the interpretation of the heavenly "signs" on or around the birth. Acknowledging that the eclipse passages are not completely preserved in each horoscope, only three of the thirteen preserved eclipses include data for magnitude, given in fingers (Texts 21 rev.1-3 and 26 rev.3-5) or in the fraction of the disk covered (Text 27). Only one horoscope (Text 27 rev. 5-8) states the time of the eclipse, noting that the moon was already eclipsed when it rose. In these features, i.e., date, zodiacal sign in which the moon was positioned when eclipsed, magnitude and time, the manner in which the eclipses are presented in the horoscope texts are not paralleled by those found in the observational genres such as diaries, goal-year texts, or the observational eclipse report compendia,[35] but in the predictive texts such as the almanacs. The eclipse recorded in horoscope Text 14 rev. 3-4 has a parallel in an almanac (LBAT *1118+ rev.10)

Table 3.1
The following eclipses are recorded in horoscopes:

Text	Birthdate (Julian)	Lunar Eclipse date (Julian)
3:5'	-297 Feb.2-5(?)	undatable due to broken context
4 r. 3-4	-287 Sep.1	-287 Nov 22
13 r.5	-223 Jul 29	undatable due to broken context
14 r.3-4	-219 Oct 21	-218 Mar 20
20 r.3-4	-125 Aug 16	passed by
21 r.1-3	-124 Oct 1	-124 Aug 24
22a r. 8'	-116 Jul 15	-116 Sep 24
22b r.14'	-114 Jun 30	-113 Jan 29
23:10-12	-87 Jan 5	-87 Mar 11
24:9-10	-82 Dec 20	

---

[34] See my ABCD, pp.36-57.

[35] Such as in LBAT 1413, *1414, 1415+1416+1417, *1419, *1420, 1421, 1426, 1427, 1437-*1450.

25:6-7	-80 Apr 22/23	-80 Apr 21
26 r.3-5	-75 Sep 4	-75 Jul 24
27 r.5-8	-68 Apr 16	-68 Sep 3

§ 3.1.4. Latitude

Statements about lunar latitude occur in three horoscopes from Uruk, texts 10 (dated -234) and 16a and b (dated -198 and -199).

Text 10:4 *sin* TA MURUB₄ *a-na* NIM *pa-ni-šú* GAR.MEŠ "The moon keeps going from the node to (increasing) positive latitude."

Text 16a:9 *sin* TA SIG KI(?) *pa-nu-šú ana* MURUB₄ GAR.MEŠ "The moon keeps going from negative latitude toward the node."

Text 16b r.10 *sin* TA LAL *ana* MURUB₄ *pa-nu-šú* GAR.MEŠ "The moon keeps going from positive latitude toward the node."

The technical terms, NIM (*šūqu*[36]) "positive latitude," SIG (*šuplu*[37]) "negative latitude," and MURUB₄ "node," point toward the language of late Babylonian astronomical texts. The lunar procedure text for System A, ACT 200,[38] contains a section for lunar latitude (column E), the first line of which reads: *epēšu ša* nim *u* sig *ša* sin *áb ana áb* 12 *dagal malak* ᵈSin 2,24 *qabalti qaqqar kiṣari* "procedure for latitude of the moon month by month. 12 (degrees is) the width of the road of the moon. 2,24 (from) the middle is the 'nodal zone'." Here, as Aaboe has pointed out,[39] the phrase "nim *u* sig," although literally meaning "high and low," becomes a technical term for positive and negative latitude. The width (dagal) of the path of the moon is stated as 12 (degrees), or 6° on either side of the ecliptic, a value which occurs in the System A lunar ephemeris column E, the atypical astronomical text (Text E obv.8-22) and is carried through to medieval astronomy.[40]

The mantic significance of celestial latitude is attested in a late Babylonian celestial omen text from Uruk:

šumma ina qaqqar DUR *maḫīri* MÚL.BABBAR *lu šūqa* (NIM) *ṣabit u* ᵈ*Ṣalbatān* ŠUL *šupul* (SIG) MÚL.UD.AL.TAR *ṣabit ina gimir ana šamê itbal lu šupul ṣabit*

---

[36] For the syllabic writing of NIM "high (positive) latitude," see LBAT 1600 rev.9'.

[37] For the syllabic writing of SIG "low (negative) latitude," see Hunger Uruk I 94: 11, 21.

[38] See Neugebauer, ACT, Vol.I, pp.186-211, and A. Aaboe and J.Henderson, "The Babylonian Theory of Lunar Latitude and Eclipses According to System A," *Archives internationales d'histoire des sciences* (1975) p.208-211.

[39] Aaboe-Henderson, "The Babylonian Theory of Lunar Latitude," p.209.

[40] Neugebauer-Sachs, "Atypical Astronomical Cuneiform Texts," JCS 21 (9167), pp.200-208, especially p.203 with note 27 for further parallels in later antiquity.

maḫīru magal DUR-*ma nišū kittu ītammū* "If Jupiter attains positive latitude in the region of the increase of the market, and Mars .... stands below Jupiter and disappears from the sky, or attains negative latitude: the market will increase and the people will speak the truth,"

and

šumma MÚL.BABBAR *utannat lu šupul ṣabit u lu itbal u* ᵈ*Ṣalbatān ba'il lu šūqa ṣabit u lu Ṣalbatānu* MÚL.BABBAR *šitqul maḫīru magal iṣehherma nišū sugâ dannu immarū* "If Jupiter is faint, or attains negative latitude, or disappears, and Mars is bright, or attains positive latitude, or Mars and Jupiter are in conjunction: the market will greatly decrease and the people will experience severe famine." [41]

§ 3.2. Solar
§ 3.2.1. Position in the Ecliptic
A solar position in the ecliptic is provided in all horoscopes except the two fifth century examples, Texts 1 and 2. Among the rest of the texts, two groups may be defined in terms of the sequence of solar and lunar longitudes. The texts from Babylon give the lunar longitude first, then immediately following, the solar. The Uruk horoscopes (Texts 5, 9, 10 and duplicate 11, and 16) all give the solar longitude immediately before the lunar, and in the case of Texts 5, 9, and 10, the solar position is given in degrees of the sign. Texts 9 and 10 from Uruk, and 27 from Babylon have degrees within the sign for the sun's position.

§ 3.2.2. Dates of Solstice or Equinox
Most horoscopes will include the date of the solstice or equinox closest to the birthdate. In fact, no solstice or equinox date is more than 2 months before or after a given birthdate (table 3.2). This makes the solstice/equinox data useful as a limiting factor for the dating of texts in which the birth date is not well preserved. The astrological significance of the nearest solstice or equinox is unknown, but the method of obtaining the relevant equinox or solstice date was that of the so-called Uruk Scheme.[42] As expected, the terminology is the same used in other late Babylonian astronomical texts, *šamáš* GUB (*izziz*) "solstice," and LÁL-*tim* (*šitqultu*) "equinox."

---

[41] Hunger Uruk I 94: 9-14, also 20-21. See the discussion in U. Koch-Westenholz, *Mesopotamian Astrology: An Introduction to Babylonian and Assyrian Celestial Divination* (Copenhagen: Carsten Niebuhr Institute Publications 19, 1995),pp.170-171.

[42] For the literature on the scheme, see Neugebauer, "A Table of Solstices from Uruk," JCS 1 (1947), pp.143-148; Neugebauer, "Solstices and Equinoxes in Babylonian Astronomy," JCS 2 (1948), pp.209-222; Neugebauer, HAMA pp. 357-363; and A. Slotsky, "The Uruk Solstice Scheme Revisited," in H. Galter, ed., *Die Rolle der Astronomie in den Kulturen Mesopotamiens* (Beiträge zum 3. Grazer Morgenlandischen Symposion, 1993), pp.359-366.

Table3.2

Text	Birthdate	Date of Sols/Equ.	months apart
1	Dar (II) X.24	WS X.9	0
4	S.E. 24 V.19	AE VI.16	1
6	S.E. 54 IX.8	WS IX.20	0
	(conception date: S.E. 53 [XII$_2$] with VE [XII$_2$].12)		
8	S.E. 61 IX.8	WS X.8	1
13	S.E. 88 V.4	SS III.30	2
14	S.E. 92 VII.12	WS IX.20	2
15	S.E. 109 XI.9	WS IX.28	2
18	S.E. 169 XII.6	VE I.4	1
19	S.E. 172 [VI].13	EA VII.2	1
20	S.E. 186 V.24	SS IV.3	1
21	S.E. 187 VI.22	AE VI.17	0
22	S.E. 195 IV.2	SS III.13	1
22	S.E. 197 IV.7	SS IV.5	0
23	S.E. 223 X.9	WS IX.28	1
25	S.E. 231 I.14/15	SS III.21	2
26	S.E. 236 V.25	SS III.16	2

§ 3.2.3. Solar Eclipses

Eclipses are found in the horoscopes, even when their occurrence did not coincide with the birthdate.[43] The evidence is too scanty to determine whether a certain relation exists between the dates of the eclipses and the birthdate. Most, however, seem to come within five months of the date of birth. A striking detail in this context is that the majority of horoscopes in which eclipses are preserved mention both lunar and solar eclipses. In particular, those which occur one-half month apart, the lunar in mid-month followed by the solar at month's end, seem to be favored.

It is well-known that goal-year texts employ the Saros eclipse cycle both to predict (lunar) eclipses and (solar) eclipse possibilities.[44] While particularly in the context of solar eclipses, the majority of which indicate that the eclipse was not seen when watched for (IGI NU PAP), the use of goal-year texts as sources for horoscopes is practically impossible to prove, the goal-year texts or diaries from which they derive are likely sources for the eclipses recorded in horoscopes. For example, the following solar eclipse appears in horoscope Text 20 rev. 4-5 (dated -124, eclipse occurred Aug. 24 -124): 28 AN.KU$_{10}$ *šamáš ina* ABSIN KI PAP NU IGI "On the 28th an eclipse of the sun in Virgo. When watched for it was not

[43] Texts 3, 4, 13, 14, 19, 20, 21, 22, 23, 24, 25, and 26.

[44] Sachs, JCS 2 (1948), pp.279, 282-3.

observed," which may be compared with this entry from a diary for -124 (LBAT 448:7'): 28 AN.KU$_{10}$ *šamáš* DIR NU P[AP] "on the 28th an eclipse of the sun, cloudy, not obs[erved]."

§ 3.3. Planetary
§ 3.3.1. Position in the Ecliptic (longitude)
The longitudes of the planets (Jupiter, Venus, Mercury, Saturn, Mars, as well as the sun and moon) are the principal data collected in horoscopes. Since the date is of primary concern, however, the planets are for the most part between synodic appearances. It is only when a planet happens to be in the same sign as the sun on the date of birth that a synodic phenomenon will be mentioned in the text.

For the most part, the longitudes are given with respect to the names of the zodiacal signs. Degrees of longitude are not common.[45]

§ 3.3.2. Synodic Phenomena
The "phases," or synodic appearances and disappearances of the planets in their traversal of the ecliptic relative to the sun, are phenomena that interested the Babylonians since the compilation of MUL.APIN, although the planetary theory in this text represents quite an early stage in its development.[46] Observation of all the synodic phenomena is attested in the astronomical diaries, where the following phenomena are recorded (designated by Greek Letter in accordance with Neugebauer's notation in ACT): For the inner planets Venus and Mercury, in sequence

Ξ   first visibility in the west (as evening star)
Ψ   first station (evening)
Ω   last visibility in the west (as evening star)
Γ   first visibility in the east (as morning star)
Φ   second station (morning)
Σ   last visibility in the east (as morning star)

For the outer planets Saturn, Jupiter, and Mars

Γ   first visibility in the east (morning rising)
Φ   fist station (morning)
Θ   acronychal rising (evening rising, roughly equivalent to opposition)
Ψ   second station (evening)
Ω   last visibility in the west (as evening star)

---

[45] See Texts 9, 10, 16a, 16b, 21, 23, and 27. See also ch.2 sub §2.1 Longitudes Table 2.2.

[46] See Hunger-Pingree, *MUL.APIN: An Astronomical Compendium in Cuneiform* (AfO Beiheft 24, 1989), pp.148-149.

With the exception of Text 1, the synodic phenomena are mentioned only on the occasion of a planet's occupying the same zodiacal sign as the sun. In this case, the planet will not be visible due to nearness to the sun. When the birth occurs during the planet's invisibility, the text expresses this with the remark "planet such-and-such is with the sun" (e.g., Text 5: 6-7 *delebat itti šamáš* GU₄ *itti šamáš* "Venus is with the sun, Mercury is with the sun") or with the statement "planet such-and-such, which had set, was not visible" (e.g., Text 6:2' GU₄.UD *šá* ⌈ŠÚ NU I⌈GI⌉). The term ŠÚ is for the last visibility (literally "setting") of a planet in the evening, in the case of an outer planet, the Greek letter phenomenon Ω, and in the case of an inner planet is an abbreviation of either ŠÚ *šá* ŠÚ "disappearance in the evening" (Ω = last visibility as evening star before inferior conjunction) or ŠÚ *šá* KUR "disappearance in the morning" (Σ = last visibility as morning star before superior conjunction.) Only occasionally is the date of a synodic event given, such as in Text 4:6-7, the last visibility (Ω) of Saturn in the evening and the last appearance of Mercury as an evening star (Ω) are dated because these occurred not very long before the birth. Text 7 upper edge 2 gives the date for Mercury's last appearance as a morning star (Σ), since this occurred on the day following the birth.

Generally speaking, the horoscopes are interested in first and last visibilities. Only Text 1, which is anomalous in every respect, records stationary points as well as "opposition."[47] Otherwise, attested synodic phenomena are limited to and distributed in the following way:

Mercury	Ξ	Ω	Γ	Σ
Venus		Ω		
Mars		Ω		
Jupiter		Ω		
Saturn		Ω		

§ 4. ASTROLOGICAL DATA

§ 4.1. *Bīt niṣirti*

A statement that the native was born in the "secret house" of a particular planet is found in a number of horoscopes.[48] Whereas the translation of this line is straightforward enough, its meaning is utterly obscure. The É (*bīt*), or KI (*ašar*), *niṣirti* is a term known from celestial omens, Neo-Assyrian royal inscriptions, and late Babylonian scientific texts as a place in which the associated planet indicates good portent.[49] The

---

[47] See Text commentary for details.

[48] See Texts 3:4', 6:4', 8 rev.2, 13 rev.6, 15 rev.3, and 18 rev.3.

[49] I have summarized the evidence in my "Elements of the Babylonian Contribution to

system correlating planets with special locations, designated by zodiacal constellations, was obviously not invented later than the seventh century. Since the system is found in the tradition of *Enūma Anu Enlil*, its roots may even extend into the second millennium.

The secret "houses" or "places" were originally general regions of constellations, not signs or degrees within signs of the zodiac. Their usage in the horoscope texts, however, seems to indicate a reference to the zodiacal sign. Six horoscopes contain reference to the "secret houses," expressed as: *ina bīt niṣirti ša* planet such-and-such *šerru alid* "the child was born in the secret house of planet such-and-such."[50] The *bīt niṣirti* becomes a datum in the horoscopic picture of the birth, and only one planetary "secret house," therefore, is mentioned in a given horoscope. Also, the position implied by the *bīt niṣirti* is never stated, as the identification of the planet's "secret house" was surely well-known. What is meant by the statement that the child was born "in the secret house" of a particular planet is the primary unknown here. We can probably assume that it was a positive statement, conveying something of good fortune for the native.

In each example (see table below), the secret house of the planet associated with the birth does not correspond to the zodiacal sign in which the particular planet was located on the date of the birth . The following chart shows the secret house of the planet given for the birth of the child in the horoscope, the zodiacal sign identified as the sign of the *bīt niṣirti*, and the sign in which the planet was located at the time of the birth.

Text	secret house of planet	secret house	longitude of planet at birth
3:4	broken		
6a:4	Mercury	Virgo	[Scorpius][51]
8 r. 2-3	Venus	Pisces	Scorpius

Hellenistic Astrology," JAOS 108 (1988), pp.53-57. In the commentary to MUL.APIN, Pingree (Hunger-Pingree, MUL.APIN, pp.146-147) suggests the *hypsoma* is implicit in the alternative names attested in this text for Saturn, i.e., MUL.*Zibanītu* "Scales" (=Libra) (or) (MUL.^d UTU) "Star of the Sun." For these passages, see MUL.APIN II i 38 and 64. The reason for Pingree's seeing in MUL.APIN early evidence for the Babylonian *hypsomata* is the identification of the *hypsoma* of Saturn as Libra, which, being 180° from Aries, rises as the sun's *hypsoma* (Aries) sets. The term *ašar niṣirti*, however, does not occur in the MUL.APIN text. See also the summary in U. Koch-Westenholz, *Mesopotamian Astrology: An Introduction to Babylonian and Assyrian Celestial Divination* (Copenhagen: Carsten Niebuhr Institute Publications 19, 1995), pp.134-136.

[50]Each horoscope employs the same formula, expressed as a complete sentence, with *šerru* as subject and *alid* as predicate, with the exception of Text 15, the predicate of which seems to have a verb ending in MEŠ.

[51] The longitude of Mercury is derived from computation only. Given in the text is only that Mercury was not visible at the birth, i.e., had set (meaning last visibility in the evening, or Ω), and that its first visibility (Γ) had "passed by." See commentary to Text 6a.

13 r. 6	Jupiter	Cancer	Scorpius
15 r.3-4	Jupiter	Cancer	Libra(?)
18 r.3-4	Jupiter	Cancer	Libra

The Babylonian *bīt* (or *ašar*) *niṣirti*'s of the planets were long ago identified as the forerunners of the Greek "exaltations" of the planets.[52] The theory of the hypsomata (ὑψώματα) in Greek astrology assigned certain longitudes in zodiacal signs as places of special influence for the planets.[53] When a planet reached a position assigned to it as a place of exaltation (or depression), it was considered to have special power (or weakness if in the depression [ταπείνωμα] 180° from the exaltation). Longitudes were assigned for the exaltations of planets in the Greek system as follows:

Sun: Aries 19°
Moon: Taurus 3°
Saturn: Libra 21°
Jupiter: Cancer 15°
Mars: Capricorn 28°
Venus: Pisces 27°
Mercury: Virgo 15°

Cuneiform evidence of the planetary *bīt niṣirti*'s, most of which, however, is Seleucid in date,[54] supplies all the identifications of *hypsomata* for the sun, moon, and five planets, and these correspond to the zodiacal signs of the Greek *hypsomata*, leaving no doubt as to the origins of the Greek theory. It also makes clear that although the literal translation of the Akkadian *bītu* in *bīt niṣirti* is "house," the term should not be confused with the later Greek astrological term "houses" (οἶκοι) and its use in Greek

---

[52] E. Weidner, "Beiträge zur Erklärung der astronomischen Keilschrifttexte," OLZ 1913, pp.208-210, and "Babylonische Hypsomatabilder," OLZ 1919, pp.10-16.

[53] See A. Bouché-Leclercq, *L'Astrologie grecque* (Paris, 1899, reprinted 1979 Scientia Verlag Aalen), pp.192-199.

[54] LBAT 1591:5-7 is the most complete list, giving heliacal risings for the planets in their *hypsomata*, see Kugler, SSB I pp.39-41 and pl.2 Nr.2. See also the text published in E.Weidner, *Gestirn-Darstellungen aus babylonischen Tontafeln*, Österreichische Akademie der Wissenschaften, Philos.-histor. Kl., S.B. 254,2 (1967), p.11, and J.P. McEwan, *Priest and Temple in Hellenistic Babylonia*, Freiburger altorientalische Studien Bd.4 (Wiesbaden, 1981), p.174-176, giving the *hypsoma* of Mercury. Finally, the text in King, STC I p.212 and II pl.69, edited by Landsberger, "Ein astralmythologischer Kommentar aus der Spätzeit babylonischer Gelehrsamkeit," AfK 1 (1923), pp.69-82. This text contains the identification of the *hypsomata* for the moon, sun, and Mars (although broken).

genethlialogy.[55] As already mentioned, the Babylonian "exaltations" differed from the Greek in that they did not correspond to degrees of longitude, but only to zodiacal constellations, or in the case of the horoscope texts, to zodiacal signs. The *bīt niṣirti*'s also differed subtly from the Greek *hypsomata* in the interpretation of their significance, i.e., not as places of greater planetary influence, but as places within which planets' positions constituted propitious omens.

The context of the *bīt niṣirti* references in the horoscopes does not suggest what meaning or use this element had in Babylonian horoscopy. On a purely descriptive level, the references are designations of particular zodiacal signs, but the significance of that sign in the context of the horoscope escapes us. From the comparison of the position occupied by the planet in whose *bīt niṣirti* the native was born, and the sign designated as the *bīt niṣirti*, as in the table above, it seems that the location of the planet on the birth date had nothing to do with the zodiacal sign corresponding to its *bīt niṣirti*. On the basis of procedures well developed in Greek astrology, Pingree raised the question whether the *bīt niṣirti* references might have something to do with the position of the moon at computed conception.[56] We have evidence in Text 7 that the date of conception was recognized as of some importance. We do not know how the Babylonians thought about the relationship between conception and birth in terms of astrological significance, as we do in Greek astrology. Ptolemy (Tetr. III.1) viewed the natural chronological starting point of a life as the time of conception and the moment of birth as only "potentially and accidentally" the starting point. He referred to these dates as "source" and "beginning." (Tetr. III.1.106) When conception date was known, it was considered to be the choice moment against which to examine the

---

[55] Ptolemy, *Tetrabiblos* I, 17, ed. and transl. F.E. Robbins (Cambridge, Mass.: Loeb Classical Library, 1940). See the discussion in A. Bouché-Leclercq, *L'Astrologie grecque* (Paris, 1899), pp.276-80 and glossary entry in O. Neugebauer and H.B.Van Hoesen, *Greek Horoscopes* (Philadelphia: *Memoirs of the American Philosophical Society* 48, 1959), p.7.

[56] In a personal communication, Pingree offered the following analysis of the meaning of the birth being "in the *bīt niṣirti* of planet x" with the caveat that given our meager evidence his hypothesis was largely guesswork.

Text	Birth: Moon	Sun	Previous Syzygy		Conception: Moon	Sun
6	Libra	Scorpius	opposition	9mo. earlier	Pisces	Virgo
8	Pisces	Sagittarius	conjunction	10 sid. mo.	Pisces	Pisces
13	Libra	Leo	conjunction	10 sid. mo.	Leo	Leo
15	end of Taurus	Aquarius	conjunction in Aquarius	9 1/2 mo.	Cancer	Cancer
18	beg. of Gemini	Pisces	conjunction	9 mo. earlier	Cancer	Cancer

situation of the heavens. The birth date was, however, inferior only in one respect. This was that "by the former (conception date) it is possible to have foreknowledge also of events preceding birth." (Tetr. III.1) Greek horoscopy begins with the determination of the ascendant point, or horoscopos. A theory attributed to "Nechepso and Petosiris"[57] indicates that the sign in which the moon was found at conception is rising at the nativity. [58] Dates of syzygies around the birth date (as well as conception?) were significant in Babylonian horoscopy, since these are given in most of the horoscopes, although the use of these data is still unknown.

§ 4.2. Predictions

In reference to the Greek horoscopes, Neugebauer and van Hoesen said, "were it not for an extensive astrological literature, the original horoscopes alone would hardly reveal their purpose to foresee the future of a person or coming events from the initial configuration of the planets."[59] The same is true of the cuneiform horoscopes. Only rarely is a personal prediction found in a horoscope.[60] Of the five horoscopes containing predictions (Texts 10 and 11 are duplicates), three stem from Uruk. The personal "predictions," formulated as omen apodoses, attest to a connection to nativity omens and to omen literature in general. Text 10 rev.1-3, for example, gives the following stock apodoses in association with "the place of Mercury": the brave one will be first in rank, he will be more important than his brothers; he will take over his father's house." In general, what few predictions are preserved concern the native's health and prosperity, obviously primary concerns of all individuals, and wholly consistent with the nature of the predictions in nativity omens. On the basis of this admittedly scanty evidence for the goal of the horoscope, the purpose of gaining divine knowledge via the heavenly phenomena at birth seems not to differ from that evidenced by the nativity omens. If one can judge the goal of these texts in terms of the knowledge finally obtained, it does not appear to be mystical, but quite pragmatic and this-worldly. In this sense, neither the omens nor the horoscopes lend themselves to an interpretation as a vehicle for mystical communication with a deity, or deities.

---

[57] On Nechepso and Petosiris, see E. Riess, *Nechepsonis et Petrosiridis fragmenta magica*, Philologus Suppl. 6 (1892), pp.325-394, and the bibliographical information provided in D. Pingree, *The Yavanajātaka of Sphujidhvaja*,vol.II (Harvard Oriental Series 48, Cambridge, Mass. and London: Harvard University Press, 1978), pp.436-437. See also the *Dictionary of Scientific Biography*, sub Petosiris.

[58] A. Bouché-Leclercq, *L'Astrologie grecque*, p.376 and 379.

[59] Neugebauer-van Hoesen, *Greek Horoscopes*, p.162.

[60] See Texts 2, 5, 9, 10, 11, and 27.

TEXTS

TEXT 1 (AO 17649)

Darius (II) Year 13, X.24 = -409 Jan. 12/13
Previous publication: Rochberg, *OrNS* 58, pp.111-114.
photo: Ibid. pl.I.
copy: Durand, *TBER* 52.

Transcription

obv.
1 ITI.AB 24 ina ZALÁG! šá 25 MU 13
2 ᴵDar-iá-a-muš LÚ.TUR a-lid
3 GAN ina 15 GU₄.UD ina NIM ár ⌜MAŠ⌝.MAŠ IGI
4 AB   AB 9 šamáš GUB 26 <KUR>
5 ZÍZ   ZÍZ DIRI KALAG ina 2 GU₄.UD ina NIM ina MÁŠ ŠÚ
6 ZÍZ 14 dele-bat ina NIM ina IGI GU ŠÚ ŠE DIRI

rev.
1 DU₆ 22 MÚL.BABBAR ina GU UŠ
2 ina ŠE 2 ina KUN ŠÚ
3 ŠU 30 GENNA ina ALLA IGI NIM TUR
4 ina 26 IGI GAN 7 UŠ AB 17 ana ME.E
5 ŠE DIRI

Critical Apparatus

obv. 3: Orthographically, the zodiacal sign for Mercury's first appearance as a morning star appears to be MAŠ.MAŠ "Gemini," and is so reflected in the copy (TBER 6 52). However, computation refutes this reading in favor of PA "Sagittarius." The sign is slightly damaged, but certainly not PA. The closest approximation would be MÁŠ "Capricorn," but Mercury was not east of ("behind") Capricorn at this point. By Mercury's last appearance as a morning star, the planet was in Capricorn (modern longitude shows Capricorn 13°, which is still acceptable after taking into consideration the +8.73° difference between modern longitudes and Babylonian ones for 410 B.C.). Line 5 therefore concurs with our computed position. For further discussion of the astronomical data, see commentary.
obv. lines 4 and 5 have an unusually large space separating the monthname and its corresponding entry.

Text 1 AO 17649

Translation

obv.

1 Ṭebētu the 24th, in the last part of night of the 25th, year 13 of
2 Darius, the child was born.
3 Kislīmu, around the 15th, Mercury's first visibility in the   east behind
(east of) Gemini.
4 Ṭebētu: (Winter) solstice was on the 9th of Ṭebētu; < last lunar
    visibility (of the month) > was on the 26th.
5 Šabaṭu: Šabaṭu, dense clouds, around the 2nd, Mercury's last
    visibility in the east in Capricorn.
6 The 14th of Šabaṭu, Venus's last visibility in the east in front (west) of
Aquarius. (The year had) an intercalary Addaru.

rev.

1 Tašrītu the 22nd, Jupiter's (2nd) stationary point in   Aquarius.
2 Around the 2nd of Addaru, (Jupiter's) last visibility in Pisces.
3 Du'ūzu the 30th, Saturn's first visibility in Cancer, (it was)
    high and faint;
4 around the 26th, (the ideal) first visibility. The 7th of Kislīmu, first
stationary point; Ṭebētu the 17th, "opposition."
5 (The year had) an intercalary month Addaru.

Commentary

    The unusual structure of this horoscope has been discussed in the
previous publication (*Or NS* 58, pp.112f.). What primarily differentiates
this text from all the others is the fact that none of the astronomical data
refer to the date of birth (X.24). This horoscope presents synodic
phenomena for all the planets except Mars and those occurring mostly
within a few months of the birth date. The exception to this is in rev. 3
where Saturn's first visibility occurs in Du'ūzu. Neither the Seleucid
sequence of planets (Jupiter, Venus, Mercury, Saturn, Mars) nor the older,
Neo-Babylonian sequence (Jupiter, Venus, Saturn, Mercury, Mars) is
followed. Instead, the order is Mercury, Venus, Jupiter, and Saturn, a
sequence not attested elsewhere. (For further discussion of planetary
sequences, see my "Benefic and Malefic Planets in Babylonian Astrology,"
in *A Scientific Humanist: Studies in Memory of Abraham Sachs* (Philadelphia,
1988), pp.323-328) , and Hunger-Pingree, *MUL.APIN*, p.147.)

Astronomical Data
obv. 3: The text gives IX.15 as the date of Mercury's first appearance as a

morning star. The reading of the zodiacal position is in doubt (see Critical Apparatus).

Computation: IX.15 = -410 Dec. 5. Solar longitude = 256.9° (modern tropical longitude); Mercury 241.84° (modern tropical). Sunrise at 3.92 UT (approximately 7:00 AM Babylonian local time); Mercury rose at 2.62 UT (approximately 5:30 AM Babylonian local time). At sunrise, Mercury's altitude was 14.28. Just before sunrise, Mercury would be low on the eastern horizon before disappearing with the light of morning. In 410 B.C., a systematic difference of 8.73° is seen between modern (tropical) and Babylonian (sidereal) longitudes. The computed position of 233.11° for Mercury should then be increased by 8.73° to find the Babylonian position, bringing Mercury to Sagittarius (rounding up, 242°).

obv. 4: The date of winter solstice here is consistent with the date generated by the Uruk Scheme (belonging to cycle -6 year 16 of the Scheme [see HAMA p.356]). The Uruk Scheme implies the use of a fixed calendar with regular intercalations now believed to have existed from about 500 B.C. (see HAMA, p.354f. and Aaboe, Britton, Henderson, Neugebauer and Sachs, "Saros Cycle Dates and Related Babylonian Astronomical Texts," TAPS 81.6 [1991], pp. 14-15 [Text C]). The date of Text 1 is approximately 30 years before the point at which the 19-year cycle is incontrovertibly in use. Exceptions to the 19-year cycle system of intercalations for the century before -380, have been reduced from two to one. Chief among the recently resolved anomalies is the intercalary year 20 of Artaxerxes II, now known to be normal and in agreement with the Saros Canon. In their joint paper, Aaboe, Britton, Hendersen, Neugebauer, and Sachs point out that PD[3]'s intercalary year of Artaxerxes II 20 is based on Strassmaier's misreading of the Saros Canon (see idem, "Saros Cycle Dates," sub Text E Critical Apparatus to Rev. IIa, 32,34 and IIb, 31,33,, p.37). The other misplaced intercalation, from year 22 of Darius (I) finds textual support (PD[3] p.7) in a Persepolis Fortification text 11424 (=OIP 92 PF 875), and possibly also Nos.1899, 5968, and 9916 (=OIP 92 PF870, 966, and 1718, for which references I thank M.W. Stolper).

obv. 5: The text gives XI.2 as the date when Mercury appears for the last time as a morning star. The zodiacal position is given as Capricorn.

Computation: XI.2 = -409 Jan. 20. Solar longitude 295.38° modern/ 304.11° Babylonian; Mercury 283.83° modern/ 292.56° Babylonian. Sunrise 4.24 UT; Mercury rises 3.59 UT. Shortly before sunrise, Mercury would be low on the eastern horizon and in the sign Capricorn.

obv. 6: The text gives XI.14 as the date of Venus' last appearance as a morning star, and gives the position as Aquarius.

Computation: XI.14 = -409 Feb.1. Solar longitude 307.42° modern/ 316.15° Babylonian; Venus 297.89° modern/ 306.62° Babylonian; sunrise 4.15 UT; Venus rises 3.67 UT. Venus therefore low on the eastern horizon just before sunrise, and in the sign Aquarius.

rev. 1: VII.22 is the date for the second station of Jupiter in Aquarius.

Computation: VII.22 = -410 Oct. 13/14. Jupiter's longitude was 313.16° modern/ 321.89° Babylonian (= Aquarius 22°) from Oct. 12 to the 16th. From the 17th it again returned to direct motion.

rev. 2: XII.2, Jupiter's last visibility in Pisces.

Computation: XII.2 = -409 Feb. 17. Solar longitude at 7:00 PM Babylonian local time 323.87° modern/ 332.6° Babylonian; Jupiter 332.98° modern/ 341.71° Babylonian (=Pisces 12°). Sunset at 14.73 UT or approximately 5:45 PM Babylonian local time. Jupiter set at 15.43 UT, and so remained visible on the western horizon for a short time after sunset before it too set. The text's date and longitude agree well with computation.

rev. 3: IV.30, Saturn's first visibility in Cancer, but said to be "high and faint."

Computation: IV.30 = -410 July 23. Solar longitude 114.21° modern/ 122.94° Babylonian; Saturn 98.55° modern/ 107.28° Babylonian (= Cancer 17°); sunrise 2.08 UT, Saturn rises .85 UT. At 2 UT, or just before sunrise, the solar altitude was -.89 and Saturn's was 12.87. The observational remark "high and faint" suggests that when Saturn was observed on IV.30 it was thought that the ideal first visibility had been missed.

rev. 4: IV.26 alternate date for first visibility of Saturn, since the planet appeared already too high on the 30th.

Computation: IV.26 = -410 July 19. Solar longitude 109.79° modern/ 118.52° Babylonian; Saturn 97.97° modern/ 106.7° Babylonian (=Cancer 17°); sunrise 2.04 UT, Saturn rises 1.11 UT, about one hour before sunrise.

rev. 5: IX.7, Saturn's first station.

rev. 6: IX.17, Saturn's "opposition," or visible evening rising.

Computation: IX.17 = -409 Jan.4. Solar longitude 279.73° modern/ 288.46° Babylonian, Saturn 103.20° modern/ 111.93° Babylonian (=Cancer 22°); elongation 176.53°. The date of true opposition would be several days later. The Babylonian "opposition" refers to the acronychal rising, or rising of the planet at sunset, which fits well with the date in the text. See A. Aaboe, "Observation and Theory in Babylonian Astronomy," *Centaurus* 24 (1980), p.35.

TEXT 2 (AB 251)

[Darius II Year 14].I.14 = -409 April 29
Previous publication: Sachs, JCS 6, p.54-57.
photo: JCS 6 pl.IV.
copy: R.C. Thompson, *A Catalogue of the Late Babylonian Tablets in the Bodleian Library, Oxford* (London, 1927), pl.2.

Transcription

obv. (Perhaps one line missing to top edge)
1 ITI(?).BARA₂ GE₆(?) 14(?) ... ... GAR(?) ÀŠ(?)
2 DUMU šá ᴵMU.ŠEŠ DUMU šá ᴵMU.MU A ᴵDe-ke-e(?) a-li[d]
3 i-nu-šú sin šap-lat SI GÍR.TAB
4 MÚL.BABBAR ina KUN.MEŠ ᵈdele-bat
5 ina GU₄.AN GENNA ina ALLA
6 AN ina MAŠ.MAŠ GU₄.UD šá Š[Ú] N[U IGI]
7 BAR 1 28 14(?) 4,40(?) [...]
8 27 U₄.NÁ.À[M]

rev.
1 ina IGI-ka ba-nu-ú [...]
2 ITI.ŠU MU.12.KAM
3 [M]U(?) 8 ..[...]
4 [...] ... [...]
Remainder broken; perhaps one line remaining to bottom edge.

Translation

1 Nisannu, night of the 14th(?), ...
2 son of Šumu-uṣur, son of Šumu-iddina, descendant of Dēkē, was born.
3 At that time, the moon was below (lit.: the lower part of) the Pincer of the Scorpion,
4 Jupiter in Pisces, Venus
5 in Taurus, Saturn in Cancer,
6 Mars in Gemini. Mercury, which had set, was not vis[ible].
7 Nisannu 1, (duration of visibility of the new crescent was) 28 (time degrees), [visibility of the moon after sunrise on) the 14th(?) was 4,40 (time degrees).
8 The last visibility of the lunar crescent was the 27th.

rev.
1 (Things?) will be propitious for you.
2 Du'ūzu, year 12,
3 [yea]r(?) 8 ...
4 [....]

Commentary

Obv.3: Because of its fifth century date, Sachs presented a detailed account of his dating of this horoscope (JCS 6 pp.54-57), and an analysis of the lunar longitude given with respect to SI GÍR.TAB, the "pincer of the Scorpion." This fixed star does not belong to the known normal stars, but MUL.APIN I ii 11, see Hunger-Pingree, MUL.APIN, p.33, provides the equivalence with the contellation Libra: MUL.ZI.BA.AN.NA SI MUL.GÍR.TAB "the Scales (=) the pincer of Scorpius." The pincers of Scorpius are also associated with Libra in the astrological text ACh Ištar 28:6-7   DIŠ MUL.GÍR.TAB SI.MEŠ-*šá zu-u'-ú-ra šá-ru-ru na-šá-a* ᵈUDU.IDIM *ina* ŠÀ MUL.*Zi-ba-ni-ti*GUB-*ma* "If the Scorpion's pincers brighten (its) body, the planet stands within the Scales." See Sachs, JCS 6 p.56 note 22 for other literature. On this basis, Sachs identified the scorpion's pincers with the northern and southern pans of the Scales, each of which constitutes a normal star, RÍN *šá* ULÚ "the southern part of the scales (= α Librae)," and RÍN *šá* SI "the northern part of the scales (= β Librae)". The lunar longitude of the horoscope is therefore interpreted to be in the vicinity of α Librae and β Librae, whose longitudes in -409 were 191.7° and 196° respectively. The astronomical data tabulated below merely confirms Sachs' original dating.

The use of *šaplâtu* "the lower part" is not found in other horoscopes, which use SIG (*šaplu*) "below" to designate the lunar position relative to a fixed star.

obv.6: Mercury had been moving retrograde and reached its greatest western elongation on the 29th of April, when it should have been at first morning rising (Γ). On the 30th, the planet returned to direct motion.

rev.: Unfortunately, the reverse of the text still presents difficulties. The analysis of the month and year stated there (rev. 2 "Du'ūzu year 12 ...") is completely obscure as to which regent it refers, as well as its relationship to the date of the birth.

Astronomical Data

λText	λ Computed (-409 Apr.29*)
moon below Pincer of Scorpion	205.38° = Libra 25°
sun omitted	40.9° = Taurus 11°
Jupiter Pisces	357.89° = Pisces 28°
Venus Taurus	53.85° = Taurus 24°
Mercury (with the sun)	19.06° = Aries 19°
Saturn Cancer	109.74° = Cancer 20°
Mars Gemini	85.73° = Gemini 26°

*Computed for 0.00 UT = 3:00 AM Babylonian local time (midnight epoch), and taking into account a discrepancy of 8.73° between modern and Babylonian longitudes for the date in question.

TEXT 3 BM 32376

TEXT 3 (BM 32376 = 76-11-17,2108)

S.E. 13 X.24-27(?) = -297 Feb. 2-5(?)
Previously unpublished

Transcription

1' [...] x x x-šú a-[lid(?)
2' [šamáš ina G]U(?) MÚL.BABBAR ina A dele-bat ina [GU(?) ŠÚ-ú]
3' [KI] ᵈUTU šú-ú U₄ 29 GU₄.U[D ina ŠÚ (ina GU) IGI(?)]
4' [GENNA ina HUN(?)] AN ina MÁŠ ina É ni-ṣ i[r-tu₄ ...]
5' [...] la-pa-ni AN.KU₁₀ s[in(?)/šamáš(?)...]
6' [...] x ⌜20⌝ [

Critical Apparatus

line 1': 3 or 4 broken signs, only bottoms preserved. The date and time of birth, as well as the lunar longitude are expected in this line. One or two more lines estimated to upper edge.
line 2': Restoration of the solar longitude is based on the unvarying sequence moon, sun, Jupiter, Venus, etc.(for discussion of the sequence of planets, see chapter 1 § 3).
line 3': The logogram ᵈUTU for the sun reflects the use of an older orthographic tradition than the writing *šamáš*, which is found more often in late astronomical texts. Cf. Text 4
(BM 33382) rev. 1, also dating to the early years of the Seleucid Era.
line 5': Though only two Winkelhaken are preserved before the break, I have read *s[in* ...] on the assumption that if *šamáš* were intended, the

logogram would be consistent with the ᵈUTU of line 3'.

Translation

1' [...] .... wa[s born(?).]
2' [The sun was in Aqua]rius, Jupiter in Leo, Venus [set] in [Aquarius],
3' it was [with] the sun. On the 29th Mer[cury's first
   appearance in the west (in Aquarius),]
4' [Saturn was in Aries(?)], Mars in Capricorn. In the *bīt niṣi[rti]*
   of ...]
5' [...] .... before the lun[ar(?)/solar(?)] eclipse [...]
6' ....

Commentary

line 3': The statement for Mercury includes the date of one of its synodic appearances, as is regularly found in the diaries and related non-mathematical astronomical texts. First visibility in the evening (expressed: planet *ina* ŠÚ *ina* zodiacal sign IGI) has been restored on the basis of modern computed data and in accordance with the terminology of the diary texts. Mercury had at approximately this time been in superior conjunction and was just becoming visible again for the first time in the west as an evening star. The table provided below shows the very good agreement between the text's data and modern computed data for year -297 with the range of dates Feb. 2-5, corresponding to the Babylonian dates Ṭebētu 24-27. Col. iii shows the data for the Julian date corresponding to "the 29th" day, associated with Mercury in obv.3', which I have restored accordingly as first appearance in the west.
line 5': The reference to the eclipse is too fragmentary to warrant much comment. It is furthermore unclear from the preserved wedges whether the eclipse was solar or lunar, although the use of ᵈUTU in the text suggests that in this line it is 30 rather than 20 following AN.KU$_{10}$. Suffice it to state that in -297 two lunar eclipses occurred, one on Dec. 14 beginning shortly after 5:00 AM Babylonian local time and lasting until after the moon set at 7:00 AM. (First contact 2.36 UT, last contact 6.14 UT or roughly just after 9:00 AM Babylonian local time), and one on June 19 beginning before the moon rose and being visible for about one hour after moonrise. A solar eclipse occurred -297 Jan. 8, beginning 3.67 UT and ending 5.55 UT. The sun rose at 6.96 or just about 7:00 AM Babylonian local time, already eclipsed, and the eclipse was over 2 1/2 hours later at approximately 9:30 AM Babylonian local time.

Dating
   The S.E. 13 date assigned to this horoscope is quite early, but has strong support for the reason that within the approximately 300-year period of the

horoscope corpus, the particular combination of the longitudes of Jupiter and Mars together with the Venus conjunction occur only in this several day period (approximately Feb. 1-6). Further agreement is found with the synodic phenomenon of Mercury's first appearance in the west and its assigned Babylonian date (the "29th").

Astronomical Data

	λ Text	λ Computed (-297 Feb. 2)*	λ Computed (-297 Feb. 7)
Sun	[Aqua]rius	316.92° = Aquarius 17°	321.92° = Aquarius 22°
Jupiter	Leo	145.04° = Leo 25°	144.39° = Leo 24°
Venus	[Aquarius]	316.36° = Aquarius 16°	322.59° = Aquarius 23°
Mercury	[Aquarius]	318.82° = Aquarius 19°	328.55° = Aquarius 29°
Saturn	[Aries]	25.85° = Aries 26°	26.22° = Aries 26°
Mars	Capricorn	279.67° = Capricorn 10°	283.51° = Capricorn 14°

* Computed for 16.00 UT = 7:00 PM Babylonian local time (midnight epoch), and adjusting by +7.18° for the difference between modern and Babylonian longitudes for the date in question.

Rising and Setting Times for the sun and Mercury (pertaining to line 3)

	-297 Feb.2		-297 Feb.7	
	Rise	*Set*	*Rise*	*Set*
Sun	4.12UT	14.52UT	4.06UT	14.60UT
Mercury	4.33UT	14.63UT	4.48UT	15.11UT

[4UT = 7AM Babylonian local time; 14UT = 5PM Babylonian local time]

TEXT 4 (BM 33382 [L*1459])

S.E.24 V.19 = -287 Sept. 1
Previously published
copy: Bertin copy 2894.

Transcription

Obv.
1 M[U 2]4.KAM ᴵSe u ᴵAn LUGAL.MEŠ
2 [ITI].⌜NE⌝ 1 U₄.14 NA GE₆ ⌜19(?)⌝
3 ⌜U₄.BI(?)⌝ sin ina IGI ŠUR GIGIR šá ULÙ
4 ⌜2⌝ KÙŠ U₄.27 KUR i-nu-šú
5 MÚL.BABBAR u dele-bat ina ALLA
6 U₄.10 GENNA ina ABSIN ŠÚ
7 U₄.14 GU₄.UD ina ŠÚ ina AB.SIN ŠÚ
rev.
1 AN ina UR.A ᵈUTU ina ABSIN
2 ITI.KIN U₄.16 LÁL-tim
one line blank
3 ITI.APIN GE₆ 13 AN.KU₁₀ sin
4 TIL-tim ina MÚL.MÚL GAR-an
5 A šá ᴵTAR-sa-mu-ku-us a-lid

Critical Apparatus

line 3: At the beginning of the line one expects U₄.BI, but traces are not
supportive of such a reading.
rev.1: Note the older conventions UR.A for A "Leo," and ᵈUTU for *šamáš*
"sun."

Translation

1 Year [2]4 (S.E.), Seleucus and Antiochus were the kings.
2 Month Abu 1, moonset after sunrise on the 14th, night of the
   [19(?)]
3 [That day(?)], the moon was to the west of "The southern ...."
   of the Chariot" (= ζ Tauri),
4 (by) 2 cubits. Last lunar visibility before sunrise was on
   the 27th. At that time,
5 Jupiter and Venus were in Cancer,
6 on the 10th Saturn's last appearance in Virgo,
7 on the 14th Mercury's last appearance in the west in Virgo,
rev.

TEXT 4 BM 33382

1 Mars in Leo, sun in Virgo.
2 Ulūlu the 16th was the (autumnal) equinox.
3 Arahsamna, night of the 13th, a lunar eclipse occurred.
4 Totality occurred in Taurus.
5 The son of Tar?-sa-mu-ku-us was born.

Commentary

line 1: The coregency of Seleucus I and Antiochus I Soter was from 20-31
S.E. (292 -281 B.C.), see PD III p.21.
line 2-4: These illustrate the use of data typical of diary texts, giving the
position of the moon with respect to a normal star on the date in question.
Note that the formulaic "at that time...," which requires planetary positions
in the zodiac follows the reference to the normal star position of the moon.
lines 6-7: Dates of Saturn's last appearance and Mercury's last visibility in
the west (both termed ŠÚ [= Ω]) are noted. The formulation is reminiscent
of almanacs. See astronomical data below.
rev. 1: The longitude of the sun is out of order, coming after Saturn,
Mercury, and Mars. Normally the sun is in second place following the
moon, but preceding all the planets.
rev. 2: Date of autumnal equinox is in accordance with the Uruk Scheme
(cycle 1 year 6, according to HAMA p.356 Table 1 and p.362 Table 3).
rev. 3-4: The lunar eclipse mentioned as occurring on Arahsamna the 13th
corresponds to the total eclipse of -287 Nov.22. The longitude of the moon
during the eclipse (of approximately 3 hours duration [21.53 UT to 1.18
UT]), specifically around totality (23.12 to 23.59 UT) was 56-57°, or Taurus
26°, which even when adjusted +7° still compares favorably enough with
the text's statement that totality occurred in Taurus.

Dating
    Although the year date is not completely preserved, the coregency
provides a narrow range between the years -291 and -280 within which the
astronomical data need to be checked. The lunar eclipse adds confirmation
to our identification of the year as -287. No time of birth is given (or at
least preserved) in the text, Because the lunar longitude is cited with respect
to a normal star, we assume the moon was above the horizon and visible.
Moonrise on V.19 (=Aug 31/Sept 1) was at 19.42UT, or approximately
10PM Babylonian local time. Computing the longitudes for 21UT
(midnight in Babylon) has the moon above the horizon (altitude 19.08).
The normal star ζ Tauri, with respect to which the moon was "2 cubits to
the west" of this star according to obv.3-4, had in the year -287 a longitude
of 53° (interpolating from the table in Sachs-Hunger, *Diaries*,p.17), which
agrees quite well with the text.

Astronomical Data

λText		λ Computed (-287 Sept.1*)
moon	2^{cu} west of ζTauri	64.34° = Gemini 4°
sun	Virgo	161.67° = Virgo 12°
Jupiter	Cancer	115.02° = Cancer 25°
Venus	Cancer	115.44° = Cancer 25°
Mercury	Virgo[1]	182.93 ° = Libra 3 °
Saturn	Virgo[2]	169.88 ° = Virgo 20 °
Mars	Leo	139.23° = Leo 19°

---

*Computed for 21.00 UT = midnight Babylonian local time, to better accommodate the lunar position with respect to normal star ζ Tauri. Computed longitudes are adjusted +7.04° for the year of the text.

Synodic Phenomena

The date for Saturn's last visibility is given as (S.E.24) V.10 = -287 Aug.24. This datum is supported by computation, which indicates a solar longitude of 153.60°, Saturn 168.90°, sunset 15.61 UT, Saturn set 16.47. At sunset, Saturn's altitude was 10.79, visible low on the western horizon.

According to the horoscope, the last appearance of Mercury as an evening star occurred on (S.E. 24) V.14. Computation supports this date, V.14 = -287 Aug.28 with a solar longitude of 157.53°, Mercury 181.86, sunset at 15.53 UT and Mercury set at 16.42 UT. At sunset, Mercury had an altitude of 11.19.

---

[1]Text does not give position of Mercury on the date of the birth, but on the date of its synodic phenomenon (Ω), when it occupied the same sign as the sun. This accounts for the small discrepancy between the longitude cited in the text and the computed longitude in the chart.

[2]The position of Saturn is also given for the date of the synodic phenomenon (Ω), rather than the date of birth.

TEXT 5

TEXT 5 (MLC 1870)
S.E. 48 XII.[23] =-262 April 4
Previous publication: Sachs, *JCS* 6, pp.57-58.
photo: *JCS* 6, pl.III.

Transcription

obv.
1 MU.48 ŠE GE₆ [ ]
2 LÚ.TUR a-lid
3 U₄.BI šamáš ina 13,30 LU
4 sin ina 10 GU
5 BABBAR ina SAG A
6 dele-bat KI šamáš
7 GU₄ KI šamáš
8 GENNA ina ALLA
9 AN ina TIL ALLA
10 [MA]Š.MAŠ HUN ù GU É ⌜x x⌝ -šú
11 [GU₄(?)] NE APIN ù ZÍZ É ŠI ṢU šú
12 [...] GU a-lid ap(?) pi šu ul lu(?)
13 [...] ⌜UD(?) na(?) na(?) an⌝ nu

14 [...] im zi(?) li [...]
15 [...] ab(?) bi ib i-tar zi(?) ⌈x x⌉
16 [...] ⌈x⌉ UD i-tar EN gi(?) ir (?)SAL(?) MEŠ
17 [...] ⌈x⌉ i-tar ra-'a-mu ú(?) [...]
18 [...] ⌈x⌉ KI-šú i-tar [...]

rev.
1 [...] i x di(?) x i-te-ep-šú
2 NÍG.ŠID LÁ-ṭí bir(?)-rat IGI^{II} KI-šú
3 i-tar ù KI ir la(?) ban(?) ⌈x⌉
4 a-kal-šú a-na bi-ru-ú ul i-[...]
5 NÍG.ŠID šá ina TUR-šú TUK-ši ul UD(?) ⌈x⌉[...]
6 MU.36.KAM NÍG.ŠID TUK-ši
7 U$_4$.MEŠ GÍD.DA
8 DAM-su šá pa-na-as-su UKÙ.MEŠ
9 i-le-'u-šu ši-i ú-še-me
10 [...].MEŠ u SAL.MEŠ TUK-ši Á.TUK IGI-ir(?)
11 [i]na bi-rit KASKAL.MEŠ a-na muh-hi NÍG.ŠID
12 [...] šá KAL

Critical Apparatus

obv. 3 Sachs' reading of the zodiacal sign LU is uncertain. The sign is
sufficiently damaged that one could read the more standard ⌈HUN⌉ as well.
Note that HUN is clearly written for Aries in line 10. On LU for Aries,
see Sachs, JCS 6 71 note 51.
obv. 11 Sachs read DU$_6$ and noted "hardly ZÍZ than anything, but I can
make no good argement for it as I do not understand the line as a whole.
obv. 12 There is the final vertical wedge of the sign in the break preserved
just before "GU." After a clear "*ul*," the sign could be DI or LU, or *lum*(?)
Rev. 1 After "i," is it a misbegotten "*tar*" sign?

Translation

obv.
1 Year 48 (S.E.), Addaru, night of the [23(?)],
2 the child was born.
3 That day the sun was in 13;30 Aries,
4 the moon in 10° Aquarius,
5 Jupiter at the beginning of Leo,
6 Venus with the sun,
7 Mercury with the sun,

8 Saturn in Cancer,
9 Mars at the end of Cancer,
10 [Gem]ini(?), Aries, and Aquarius: the house(?) of his ....
11 [(month name) (?)], Abu, Arahsamna, and Šabaṭu: the house(?) of his ....
12 [...] .... was born ....
13-16 (too damaged for translation)
17 [...] love(?) ....
18 .... he will return (?) [to?] his place [...]

rev.
1 [...] .... they made.
2 He will be lacking property, ...
3 ....
4 His food(?) will not [suffice(?)] for his hunger(?).
5 The property which he had acquired in his youth(?) will not [last(?)].
6 The 36th year (or: 36 years) he will have property.
7 (His) days will be long.
8-9 His wife, whom people will seduce(?) in his presence, will .... (or: His wife, in whose presence people will overpower him, she will bring (it) about(?).)
10 He will have ...'s and women. He will see(?) profit.
11 Between travels concerning property
12 [...] ....

Commentary

obv. 3-4: The use of degrees within the zodiac for the moon, instead of the number of cubits with respect to a normal star, and also fractions of degrees for the ecliptical longitude of the sun is rare. See also texts 9, 10, 16, and 22.

Astronomical Data

	λ Text	λ Computed (-262 Apr. 4)*
moon	Aquarius 10°	311.38 = Aquarius 11°
sun	Aries 13;30°	16.28 = Aries 16°
Jupiter	beginning of Leo	121.47 = Leo 1°
Venus	with the sun	15.15 = Aries 15°
Mercury	with the sun	4.19 = Aries 4°
Saturn	Cancer	103.79 = Cancer 14°
Mars	end of Cancer	110.04 = Cancer 20°

*Computed for 1.00 UT, or approximately 4:00 AM Babylonian local time, adjusting computed longitudes +6.7° for the date in question.

TEXT 6 BM 47721

TEXT 6 (BM 47721 = 81-11-3,426)

(a) [S.E.53 VIII.24] = -258 Nov. 14/15
(b) S.E.61 II.8 = -250 May 5/6
Previously unpublished

Transcription

obv.(flat side)
1' ᵣa-lid ina si-man-ni-šú˺ x [6-7 signs]
2' GENNA ina ABSIN AN ina MÁŠ GU₄.UD šá ᵣŠÚ-ú NU I˺GI U₄.n(?)]
3' GU₄.UD ina NIM UD.DA ŠÚ-šú DIB U₄.15 NA
4' 27 KUR ina É ni-ṣir-tu₄ šá GU₄.UD a-lid

---

lower edge uninscribed
rev.(rounder side)
1 [MU.K]U.1.KAM ᴵAn-ti-'u-uk-su LUGAL
2 [ITI.G]U₄ 30 GE₆ 8 SAG GE₆ sin ár DELE šá IGI ABS[IN(?)]
3 [...] KÙŠ U₄ 8 šá 30 DANNA ME ana ᵣŠÚ˺ šamáš a-lid [...]
4 [ina si-ma]-ni-šú ᵈsin x x x x [...]
remainder broken

Critical Apparatus

   More than one horoscope is recorded on this tablet. The width of the lines is also greater than most.
obv. 1': Transliteration of this line is uncertain since only the bottoms of signs are visible. Expected in this space are positions of the moon, sun, Jupiter and Venus.
rev. 4: After ᵈsin, only bare traces of wedges.

Translation

obv.
1' [was born. In his hour (of birth), the moon was in ...,] [sun in ..., Jupiter in...,
      Venus in ...,]
2' Saturn in Virgo, Mars in Capricorn, Mercury which had set was
      not vis[ible. On the nth,]
3' Mercury's first visibility in the east, its setting passed by.
      Moonset after sunrise occurred on the 15th [...]
4' the last lunar visibility on the 27th. In the *bīt niṣirti* of
      Mercury he was born.

rev.

1 [Year] 61 (S.E.), Antiochus(II) was king.
2 [Aj]aru 30, night of the 8th, beginning of night, moon
   east of the Single star in the front of the Fur[row] (= γ Virginis]
3 [by n] cubits. The 8th day, at one-half *bēru* before sunset,
   he was born [...]
4 [in] his [ho]ur (of birth), the moon .... [...]
remainder broken

Commentary

obv. 2: Cf. LBAT 1251:25.

rev. The date of horoscope (b) is well preserved and the astronomical phenomena computed for this date is provided below (see table of astronomical data for horoscope (b).

rev. 2-3: Note the position of the moon, cited with respect to the normal star, east of γ Virginis, or about 159.2° (in -250, the longitude interpolated from the values for -300 and 0 given in Sachs-Hunger, *Diaries*, p.18), and stated as being at the time SAG GE$_6$ "beginning of night" (beginning of night of Ajaru 8 = May 4 approximately 17 UT, or 8PM Babylonian local time). Such normal star references are frequently given in the diaries in this form, SAG GE$_6$ being a common time designation in these contexts. The lunar position does not, however, correspond to the time of the birth, which is stated in line 3 as the number of *bēru* "ME *ana* ŠÚ" meaning the amount of daylight until sunset. The lunar position was probably obtained from the diary corresponding to the date of the birth, and the discrepancy of the time of birth was not of concern. According to the text, the birth occurred one hour before sunset on Ajaru 8 (=May 5), i.e., approximately 15 UT (approximately 6 PM Babylonian local time).

Horoscope (a) Dating
   Very few astronomical data are preserved here, and there are no other limiting factors with which to narrow the date. All one has are the longitudes of Saturn and Mars, the fact that Mercury "had set" (Ω), i.e., was at inferior conjunction, and , in line 3', that Mercury's first visibility in the east (Γ) occurred, possibly on a date broken at the end of line 2'.
   One possible fit is year -230 (S.E. 81), but with this date, if the tablet's flat side is indeed the obverse, the horoscope recorded first would be for a birth that occurred twenty years *after* that recorded subsequently. If the horoscopes are to be in chronological sequence, a date -258 (S.E. 53) is workable, and the horoscopes are also not separated by very many years. The year and month may be secured by the extant planetary data. If the date is to be further specified by the fact that Mercury has passed inferior conjunction (Ω) and is somewhere either approaching or also passed first

visibility (Γ), the birth probably fell between Nov. 10 and 20. Without further evidence from the horoscope, and failing parallel material from non-mathematical astronomical texts, we cannot improve on this dating. On this basis, the data listed below are computed for Nov. 15.

Horoscope (a) Astronomical Data

	λ Text	λ Computed (-258 Nov. 15)*
moon	[ ]	209.31° = Libra 19°
sun	[ ]	236.48° = Scorpius 26°
Jupiter	[ ]	259.72° = Sagittarius 20°
Venus	[ ]	220.13° = Scorpius 10°
Mercury	(with the sun)	237.48° = Scorpius 27°
Saturn	Virgo	173.01° = Virgo 23°
Mars	Capricorn	286.79° = Capricorn 17°

*Computed for 16 UT, or 7 PM Babylonian local time. Computed longitudes are adjusted +6.64 for -258.

Horoscope (b) Dating

Obviously, the only astronomical datum preserved in the text is the position of the moon given with respect to the normal star γ Virginis, which had a longitude of 159.2° in -250. The computed position of the moon is 155° which is 4° *west* of the longitude of the normal star, although the text has the moon some (not preserved) amount of cubits *east* of the normal star. The date of the horoscope, however, is preserved, as is the time of the birth, which came at the end of the day Ajaru 8 (= May 6), while the lunar position is cited for the beginning of Ajaru 8, i.e., "beginning of night." The lunar position is therefore computed for Ajaru 8 shortly after sunset, or the beginning of night, which corresponds to May 5 in the Julian calendar.

Horoscope (b) Astronomical Data

Only the lunar longitude has been computed, since there are no data preserved in the text to be compared with computed longitudes.

	λ Text	λ Computed (-250 May 4*)
moon	east of γ Virginis n^{cu}	154.84° = Virgo 5°

*Computed for 16.00 UT to correspond with "beginning of night." Sunset was 15.56 UT. The computed longitude reflects an adjustment of +6.53° for -250.

Text 7 BM 33667

TEXT 7 (BM 33667)

S.E. 54 IX.8 =-257 Dec. 15
Previous publication: Kugler, *SSB* II 558-562; republished in Sachs, *JCS* 6, pp.58-60.
photo: *JCS* 6, pl.IV.
copy: Schaumberger (recopied from Strassmaier), *SSB* Erg.3, Taf.VII, Nr.14.

Transcription

obv.
1 MU.53 ⌜x⌝ GE$_6$ 1 30
2 SIG MUL IGI šá SAG HUN 2 1/2 KÙŠ [...]
3 U$_4$.12 LÁL-tim
4 U$_4$.1.KAM 30 ZIB.ME [x]

rev.
1 MU.54 GAN 1 GE$_6$ 8
2 SAG GE$_6$ sin SIG Nu-nu 1 1/2 K[ÙŠ(?)]
3 sin 1/2 KÙŠ ana NIM DIB
4 U$_4$.20.KAM ^{d}UTU GUB
5 13 11 NA(?) šá ^{d}sin

Upper edge
1 i-nu-šú MÚL.BABBAR ina MÁŠ dele-bat ina GÍR.TAB
2 ina 9 GU$_4$.UD ina NIM ina PA ŠÚ
3 GENNA u AN ina RÍN

Critical Apparatus

obv. 1 The half preserved sign or signs following the year number are discussed by Sachs, JCS 6 p.58 in the critical apparatus. His comment "no obvious reading results," unfortunately, remains the case. But because of the date of vernal equinox given in line 3, one expects ŠE.DIRI.

Translation

obv.
1 Year 53 (S.E.), [intercalated (month Addaru)(?)], night of the 1st, the moon
2 (passed) below the front star of the head of the Hired Man (β Arietis) 2 1/2 cubits.
3 (Vernal) equinox was on the 12th day.

4 The 1st day, the moon .... Pisces.

rev.
1 Year 54 (S.E.), Kislīmu 1, night of the 8th,
2 beginning of night, the moon was 1 1/2 cubits below (the
      bright star of the Ribbon of) the Fishes (η (?) Piscium),
3 the moon passed 1/2 cubit to the east.
4 The (winter) solstice was on the 20th day.
5 The 13th day, 11 (UŠ) was the (duration of) the NA of the moon (=lunar
visibility after
      sunrise).

Upper edge
1 At that time, Jupiter was in Capricorn, Venus in Scorpius,
2 on the 9th, Mercury appeared for the last time in the east
      in Sagittarius,
3 Saturn and Mars were in Libra.

Astronomical Data

Sachs pointed out (*JCS* 6 p.59), that Kugler (SSB II pp.354-362)
recognized that this horoscope gives both the date of birth (rev. 1: S.E. 54
IX.8 = -257 Dec. 15) and of conception (obv. 1: S.E. 53 XII₂.1 = -257
March 17). Since the duration of pregnancy in this case is 273 days, as Sachs
said, it is "virtually the mean value of 273 1/3 days proposed in Greek
astrological compositions." (*JCS* 6, p.59 and note 29 citing A. Bouché-
Leclercq, *L'Astrologie grecque* (Paris, 1899), p.380).

The astronomical data on the conception date includes the lunar
position with respect to a normal star: 2 1/2 cubits below β Arietis. In
-257, β Arietis had a longitude of 9.23° (this value reflects interpolation
from the values for the longitude of this fixed star for -300 and 0 given in
Sachs-Hunger, *Diaries*, p.17, and the adjustment +6.63° for comparison
with ancient values). Computation shows the moon at λ10.67°. In
addition, the vernal equinox date S.E. 53 XII₂.12 (obv. 3) is in agreement
with the Uruk Scheme as well as being the closest solstice or equinox date
to the date of conception.

On the birth date, the lunar longitude is to be compared with that of η
Piscium. Interpolating from the values in Sachs-Hunger, *Diaries*, p.17, η
Piscium had a longitude of 2.13° (= 355.5° adjusted +6.63 for comparison
with ancient data) in -257. See the table below for the computed longitude
of the moon.

The date of winter solstice occurred inthe month of the birth and was
so noted in the horoscope. The date is also in accordance with the Uruk
Scheme.

The data for Mercury and the sun are omitted for the date of the birth, but Mercury's last appearance as a morning star (*ina* NIM ŠÚ) in Sagittarius on the day following the birth (IX.9) is given. See below for the risings, altitudes, and longitudes of the sun and Mercury at Σ for the date in question (= Dec. 16).

Astronomical Data

	λText	*λ Computed (-257 Dec. 15*)*
moon	1 1/2ᶜᵘ below η Piscium	3.49 = Aries 3°
sun	omits	
Jupiter	Capricorn	293.25 = Capricorn 23°
Venus	Scorpius	226.14 = Scorpius 16°
Mercury	omits	
Saturn	Libra	186.03 = Libra 6°
Mars	Libra	192.59 = Libra 12°

---

*Computed for 14.00 UT = sunset, which occurred on that date at about 5:00 PM Babylonian local time. This is meant to correspond to the text's "beginning of night" (rev.2). Computed longitudes are adjusted +6.63° for -257.

The table below for Mercury and the sun shows that at approximately one-half hour before sunrise, while the sun was still below the horizon (indicated by negative altitude values), Mercury was very low on the eastern horizon. The planet was at 12° elongation on the 16th, and progressively nearing the sun at superior conjuntion. The text states the longitude as Sagittarius, and the computation shows 255.63° (= Sagittarius 15°).

	-257 Dec. 16*			-257 Dec. 17*		
	rise (UT)	altitude	λ	rise (UT)	altitude	λ
sun	4.08	-6.62	260.70°	4.09	-6.75	261.72 °
Mercury	3.21	3.26	248.99°	3.29	2.57	250.54 °

---

* Computed for 3.50 UT, or about one-half hour before sunrise in Babylon. These longitudes have not been adjusted.

TEXT 8   BM 36943

TEXT 8 (BM 36943 = 80-6-17, 644)

S.E. 61 IX.8 = -250 Nov. 28/29
Previously unpublished

Transcription

obv.
up edge [   ] traces [   ]
1 [   ] x x x [   ]
2 [SIG?] ⌜MÚL⌝ KUR šá DU[R(?) nu-nu]
3 [   ] traces [   ]
4 ina(?) si(?)-ma(?)-ni(?)-šú ᵈ[sin ina LU(?)...]
5 ᵈUTU ina PA MÚL.BABBAR ina [ABSIN]
6 dele-bat ina ⌜GÍR.TAB⌝ AN ina RÍN
7 GENNA u GU₄.UD šá ŠÚ-ú
8 ⌜NU IGI.MEŠ(?)⌝ KI šamáš šú-nu
9 [I]TI.BI 15 NA 27 ⌜KUR⌝
rev.
1 [M]U.BI ITI.AB 8
2 [šamáš] GUB ina É ni-ṣir-tu₄
3 šá dele-bat LÚ.TUR a-lid
remainder uninscribed

Critical Apparatus

obv. top could be traces, or nothing.
obv.5: Badly preserved KI.HAL (ABSIN) also looks like ZIB.ME, although computation argues in favor of the reading ABSIN.
obv. 6: End of the line, RÍN looks secure, but the position of Mars in Libra is the only one not supported by computation. Perhaps read MÚL, for Taurus?

Translation

obv.
1 ....
2 ....
3 [(the moon was) [below?] the bright star of the Rib[bon of the Fishes (= η Piscium)]
4 ....
5 in his hour (of birth), [the moon was in Aries(?)]
6 sun in Sagittarius, Jupiter in Virgo
7 Venus in Scorpius, Mars in Libra,

8 Saturn and Mercury which had set
9 were not visible, they were with the sun.
10 That month, moonset after sunrise was on the 15th, the last
    lunar visibility was on the 27th.
rev.
1 That [year] Ṭebētu.8 was the date of
2 (winter) solstice. In the *bīt niṣirti*
3 of Venus, the child was born.

Commentary

obv. 3: The normal star position of the moon refers to MÚL KUR *šá* DUR *Nu-nu* "the bright star of the ribbon of the fishes," or η Piscium. In -250 η Piscium had a longitude of 2.09° (= 355.56° + 6.53° adjusting for ancient longitudes). Cf. the table of astronomical data below for the lunar longitude on the date restored for this horoscope.
rev.1-2: Winter solstice on X.8 belongs to the Uruk Scheme, year 5.

Astronomical Data

	λ Text	λ Computed (-250 Nov.28*)	
moon	[below η Piscium]	357.37	= Pisces 27°
sun	Sagittarius	249.7	= Sagittarius 10°
Jupiter	Virgo	164.48	= Virgo 14°
Venus	Scorpius	237.04	= Scorpius 27°
Mercury	(with the sun)	234.01	= Scorpius 24°
Saturn	(with the sun)	255.88	= Sagittarius 16°
Mars	Libra	54.47	= Taurus 24°

*Computed for 16.00 UT = 7:00 PM Babylonian local time (midnight epoch), and corrected +6.53° for the year date.

TEXT 9 NCBT 1231

TEXT 9 (NCBT 1231)

63 S.E. X.2 = -248 Dec.29
Previous publication: Paul-Alain Beaulieu and F. Rochberg, "The Horoscope of Anu-bēlšunu," JCS (forthcoming)
photo:

Transcription

obv. (rev. uninscribed)
1 [MU].1,3.KAM ITI.AB GE₆ U₄ 2.KAM
2 [ⁱ]ᵈ60.EN-šú-nu a-lid
3 U₄.BI šamáš ina 9,30 ina MÁŠ
4 sin ina 12 GU U₄.ME-šú GÍD.MEŠ
5 BA[BBAR] ina SAG GÍR.TAB mam-ma NUN qát-[su DIB]-bat
6 [LÚ.TUR(?)]ˈxˈ GU KI dele-bat a-lid ˈDUMUˈ.MEŠ TUK
7 [GU₄.U]D ina MÁŠ \\ GENNA ina MÁŠ
8 [AN] ina ALLA

Critical Apparatus

line 5: Restoration of BA[BBAR] is justified by the traces, but also by necessity of the order in which the planetary positions are cited in horoscope texts. See above, pp. 9-10 for discussion.
line 6: After the break before GU one expects *ina*, but trace is of a Winkelhaken followed by perhaps two vertical wedges. The reading of this

line remains uncertain.

Translation

1 Year 63 Ṭebētu evening of(?) day 2
2 Anu-bēlšunu was born.
3 That day, the sun was in 9;30° Capricorn,
4 moon was in 12° Aquarius: His days will be long.
5 [Jupiter] was in the beginning of Scorpius: someone will help the prince.
6 [The child(?)] was born [i]n(?) Aquarius with/ or in the region of(?) Venus: He will have sons.
7 [Merc]ury was in Capricorn; Saturn in Capricorn;
8 [Mars] in Cancer

Commentary

obv. 1: The formulation of the date of birth is not entirely clear because of the juxtaposition (redundancy?) of GE$_6$ "night" and U$_4$ "day." Whereas the horoscopes were not formulated in any standard way, the births are usually noted as occurring on the "night of ...," or the "day of ...," as in Texts 21 and 26.
obv. 2: The Anu-bēlšunu of this horoscope is identifiable as Anu-bēlšunu, son of Nidintu-Anu, descendant of Sîn-leqe-unninni, and father of Anu-aba-utēr, known as a scribe of *Enūma Anu Enlil* and copyist of the well known astrological text with depictions of constellations, published in Weidner, *Gestirn-Darstellungen aus babylonischen Tontafeln*, (Vienna, 1967). Anu-bēlšunu's name appears in the colophons of a number of astronomical texts, spanning the years S.E.118 to S.E. 124, see Neugebauer ACT 13-26 for colophons E, F, H and L (as father of Anu-aba-utēr), M, Q, R,T, U, Y (as father of Anu-aba-utēr), Z, Zb, and Zc, Zd, Ze (all as father of Anu-aba-utēr). According to the date of birth given in the horoscope, Anu-bēlšunu would have been between the ages of 55 and 61 at the writing of these astronomical documents. See also the ritual tablet copied by Anu-bēl-šunu and son Anu-aba-utēr, published by W. Mayer, "Seleukidische Rituale aus Warka mit Emesal-Gebeten," OrNS 47 (1978), p.441.
obv. 3 For other horoscopes giving fractions of degrees for the solar longitude, see texts 5:3, and 10:3. Note that these two horoscopes are also from Uruk.
obv. 4: The lunar longitude confirms the time of birth fairly well.

Astronomical data

	λ Text	λ Computed (-248 Dec. 29)*
Sun	9;30° Capricorn	281.8 = Capricorn 12°
Moon	12° Aquarius	315.39 = Aquarius 15°
Jupiter	beginning of Scorpius	221.65 = Scorpius 12°
Venus	Aquarius	313.4 = Aquarius 13°
Mercury	Capricorn	294.95 = Capricorn 25°
Saturn	Capricorn	279.58 = Capricorn 10°
Mars	Cancer	93.25 = Cancer 3°

*Computed for 16 UT, or about 7:00 PM Babylonian local time (midnight epoch), and adjusted +6.5° for the year of the text.

TEXT 10 MLC 21

Text 10 (MLC 2190)

S.E. 77 III.4 =-234 June 2/3
Previous publication: Sachs, *JCS* 6, pp.60-61.
photo: *JCS* 6 pl.III.

Transcription

obv.
1 MU.1,17 SIG 4 ina ZALÁG 5
2 ¹A-ri-is-tu-ug(?)-gi-ra-te-e a-lid
3 U₄.BI sin ina A šamáš ina 12,30 ina MAŠ.MAŠ
4 sin TA MURUB₄ ana NIM pa-ni-šú GAR.MEŠ
5 BE-ma TA MURUB₄ a-na NIM pa-ni-šú GAR.MEŠ
6 SIG₅ rab-bu-tú MÚL.BABBAR ina 18 PA UŠ
7 KI MÚL.BABBAR GI-át SILIM-át NÍG.TUK SUMUN-bar
8 U₄.MEŠ GÍD.DA.MEŠ dele-bat ina 4 MÚL.MÚL
9 KI dele-bat e-ma GIN-ku ŠE.GA
10 DUMU.MEŠ u DUMU.SAL.MEŠ TUK-ši GU₄.UD ina MAŠ.MAŠ
(4 lines uninscribed to bottom edge)

rev.
1 KI šamáš KI GU₄.UD qar-ra-du
2 SAG.KAL-du-tú GIN.MEŠ
3 UGU ŠEŠ.MEŠ-šú DUGUD-it É AD-šú EN!-el
4 GENNA 6 ALLA AN 24 ALLA KAR(?).MEŠ
5 22 23 šá ITI-us-su me-si-šú
remainder uninscribed

Critical Apparatus

obv. 6 Read SIG₅ instead of šah, and cf. duplicate Text 11:6.
rev. 3   End of line, the verb appears to be written BE-*el*, perhaps in
phonetic anticipation of the inflected form *ibêl*. Cf. Text 11 rev.4.
rev. 5   Read after *arhussu* ME-si-šú, after the duplicate Text 11 rev. 7.
Meaning is quite obscure. See also Sachs' comment JCS 6 p.60 under
Critical Apparatus.

Translation

obv.
1 Year 77 (S.E.), Simanu the 4th, in the morning(?) of the
   5th(?)

2 Aristocrates was born.
3 That day, the moon was in Leo, sun was in 12;30 Gemini.
4 The moon goes with increasing positive latitude (literally:
   "sets its face from the middle (nodal zone) toward positive latitude":
5 "If (the moon) sets its face from the middle toward positive latitude,
6 prosperity (and) greatness." Jupiter in 18° Sagittarius.
7 The place of Jupiter: (the native's life[?] will be) prosperous, at peace(?);
his wealth will be long-lasting,
8 long days (i.e., life). Venus was in 4° Taurus.
9 The place of Venus: he will find favor wherever he goes;
10 he will have sons and daughters. Mercury in Gemini,
(approximately 4 lines uninscribed)

rev.
1 with the sun. The place of Mercury: the brave one
2 will be first in rank;
3 he will be more important than his brothers; he will take over
  his father's house.
4 Saturn in 6° Cancer. Mars in 24° Cancer. ....
5 the 22nd and 23rd of each month ....
remainder uninscribed

Commentary

obv. 4: The expression *sin* TA MURUB₄*ana* NIM *pa-ni-šú* GAR.MEŠ "the
moon sets its face from the middle (MURUB₄ = *qablītu* "nodal zone")
toward positive latitude (NIM)," was borne out by Sachs' computation, see
JCS 6, p.61 commentary.   This terminology reflects that of the
astronomical ephemerides in which NIM *u* SIG "above and below (the
ecliptic)" are technical terms for positive and negative lunar latitude.
Alone, NIM can be used for positive latitude and SIG for negative, see ACT
200 obv.I 26, and Neugebauer and Sachs, "Some Atypical Astronomical
Cuneiform Texts. I," JCS 21 (1967), Text E passim, pp.200-208. See also A.
Aaboe and J. Henderson, "The Babylonian Theory of Lunar Latitude and
Eclipses According to System A, " *Archives Internationales d'Histoire des
Sciences* 25 (1975), pp.181-222.
obv.6: Instead of the problematic substantive *šahrabbūtu* (JCS 6, p.60), one
can read two substantives, SIG₅ (*dumqu*) "prosperity" and *rabbûtu*
"greatness". This lunar omen, with its prediction seemingly in reference to
an individual (at least it does not refer explicitly to the king), may reflect a
nativity omen not otherwise yet known.
  As Sachs commented, p.61 note 32, the UŠ at the end of the line ought
to be "stationary point," but would be very far off the date of the rest of the
phenomena, by 50 days too late if first station, and 60 days too early if

second station.

obv. 7-13: Personal predictions according to the KI (*qaqqaru*) "place" of the planets are paralleled in nativity omens. Note also the parallels to *ēma illaku magir* in BRM 4 24:48 and 64, and KAR 228:18. See Sachs, *JCS* 6, p.61 note 33 and Appendix II obv. 29-30. See also my "Mixed Traditions in Late Babylonian Astrology," *ZA* 77 (1987), pp.207-228.

The reading of GI is far from certain. Although *šalāmu* is permissible according to lexical lists (A III/1:243, cited CAD s.v. *šalāmu* lexical section), it is not usual in our context. Rather, the writing GI for *šalāmu* occurs typically in Neo-Babylonian personal names. However, the usage "to be successful, to prosper" (CAD s.v. meaning 4) seems appropriate. The only parallels known to me are JCS 6 66:35 (KIN NU GI) and TCL 6 13 obv. right hand col. lines 1 and 4 (KIN NU GI).

Reading DI as SILIM = *salāmu* is also problematic. The sense of the G-stem, "to become reconciled, to make peace," does not work in this context, where the verb should function as a predicate adjective modifying the life of the native, something like "(his life) will be of a peaceful nature," or "characterized by reconciliation (as opposed to strife)."

Astronomical Data

Computation has been made for June 3 at about one hour before sunrise (which was 1.92 UT on this date). The date and time indication found in line 1 of the horoscope, however, presents difficulties. The meaning of "4 ina ZALÁG 5" is uncertain, since the border between days 4 and 5 is not morning, but evening. "Toward morning" of the 5th day would be preceded, not by the 4th, but by a full one-half of the 5th day, i.e., from sunset to sunrise. As already noted by Sachs (*JCS* 6, p.61 note 31), the lunar longitude is not precise enough to be of help in resolving the time of birth.

	λ Text	λ Computed (-234 June 3*)		
moon	Leo	26.09°	=	Leo 6°
sun	Gemini 12;30°	73.49°	=	Gemini 13°
Jupiter	Sagittarius 18°	260.05°	=	Sagittarius 20°
Venus	Taurus 4°	27.85°	=	Aries 28°
Mercury	Gemini (with sun)	52.15°	=	Taurus 22°
Saturn	Cancer 6°	90.48°	=	Cancer 0°
Mars	Cancer 24°	115.60°	=	Cancer 26°

*Computed for 1.00 UT = 4:00 AM Babylonian local time (midnight epoch), and adjusted +6.31° for -234.

TEXT 11 (W 20030/143)

S.E. 77 III.4 = -234 June 2/3
copy: BagdM. Beih. 2 82

Transcription

obv.
1 [MU.1,17 SIG 4 ina ZALÁG] ⌜5⌝
2 [ᴵA-r]i-is-tu-ug-ra-te-e a-lid
·3 [U]₄.BI sin ina A šamáš ina 12,30 MAŠ.MAŠ
4 sin TA MURUB₄ ana NIM pa-ni-šú GAR.MEŠ
5 BE-ma TA MURUB₄ a-na NIM
6 pa-ni-šú GAR.MEŠ SIG₅ rab-bu-tú
7 MÚL.BABBAR ina 18 PA U⌜Š KI⌝ MÚL.BABBAR
8 GI-át DI-át NÍG.TUK SUMUN-bar U₄.MEŠ
9 [G]ÍD.DA.MEŠ dele-bat ina 4 MÚL.MÚL
10 ⌜KI⌝ Dil-bat e-ma DU-ku ŠE.GA
11 [DUMU.MEŠ u DUMU.SAL].MEŠ TUK-ši
12 [GU₄.UD ina MAŠ.M]AŠ KI šam[áš]

rev.
1 [KI GU₄.UD] qar-[ra-du]
2 [SAG.KAL]-du-tú DU.MEŠ
3 UGU ŠEŠ.MEŠ DUGUD-it
4 ⌜É⌝ AD-šú EN!-el
5 [GENN]A 6 ALLA AN 24 ALLA KAR.MEŠ
6 22 24-šú ITI-us-su
7 me-si-šú

Critical Apparatus

rev. 4 The verb appears to be BE-el, and the text needs collation. The
duplicate MLC 2190 rev.3 has the same in this passage. In the duplicate,
neither sign EN nor BE is very clear, but EN-el (*ibêl*) makes some sense in
this context. The scribe may in fact have written BE, unintentionally
reflecting the verb *bêlu* phonetically.

For Translation, Commentary, and Astronomical Data, see Text 10.

TEXT 12   BM 33741

TEXT 12 (BM 33741)

S.E. 82 III.28 = -229 July 2
Previous publication: Sachs, *JCS* 6, pp.61-62.
photo: *JCS* 6, pl.III.

Transcription

obv.
1 [M]U.1,22.KAM ITI.SIG GE₆ [...]
2 U₄(?) 28.KAM ᶦNik-(?)-nu-ú-ru
3 a-lid U₄.BI sin ina SAG ALLA
4 šamáš ina ALLA MÚL.BABBAR ina MAŠ.MAŠ
5 ˹dele-bat ina MAŠ.MAŠ ...˺
remainder, appearing to be almost half the tablet, broken.

Critical Apparatus

   See JCS 6, p.62 for comments on uncertain readings. The inscription on
the reverse ends with the preserved half of the tablet. Only one or two tails
of verticals are still visible.

Translation

1 [Ye]ar 82 (S.E.), Simanu, night [...]
2 28th day(?), Nikanor(?)
3 was born. That day, the moon was in the beginning of Cancer,

4 the sun was in Cancer, Jupiter was in Gemini,
5 [Venus was in Gemini ...]
remainder broken

Commentary

obv. 2: G.J.P. McEwan, *Priest and Temple in Hellenistic Babylonia* (FAOS 4, 1981), p.26 cites a temple official named Bēl-ibni, *šatammu* of Esagila during the years S.E.75-85, also called ^{lú}*paqdu* ^I*Ni-ka-nu-ru* "deputy of Nikanor" (CT 49 118:2; 122:3). If this reference should prove to be connected to the Nikanor of the present horoscope, we have a small bit of evidence for our supposition that those who commisioned horoscopes were in a position to do so by rank, as well as by being in contact with the temple scribes who constructed the horoscopes.

Dating
    S.E. 82 III.28 corresponds to the Julian calendar dates -229 July 1-2. The horoscope does not give a time of birth, or it is not preserved, so I have used the lunar longitude as an indication of time and computed for the date corresponding to approximately noon of III.28 falls on July 2.

Astronomical Data

	λ Text	λ Computed (-229 July 2*)	
moon	beginning of Cancer	92.57°	= Cancer 2°
sun	Cancer	101.19°	= Cancer 11°
Jupiter	Gemini	69.09°	= Gemini 9°
Venus	[...]	71.44°	= Gemini 11°
Mercury	[...]	81.79°	= Gemini 22°
Saturn	[...]	152.79°	= Virgo 3°
Mars	[...]	67.43°	= Gemini 7°

---

*Computed for 9.00 UT, or about noon Babylonian local time (sun rose at 1.91 UT), and adjusted +6.24° for -229.

TEXT 13 (BM 47642 = 81-11-3,347)

S.E. 88 V.4 = -223 July 29
Previously unpublished

Transcription

obv.
1 [MU].⌈1,⌉ 28.KAM ᴵSe-lu-ku LUGAL
2 [ITᵀ]I.NE 30 GE₆ 4 SAG GE₆ sin
3 SIG SA₄ šá ABSIN 1 5/6 KÙŠ sin 1/2 KÙŠ
4 ana NIM DIB U₄.4.KAM LÚ a-lid
5 ina si-ma-ni-šú ᵈsin ina RÍN
6 ᵈUTU ina A MÚL.BABBAR u GENNA
7 ina GÍR.TAB dele-bat ina MAŠ.MAŠ GU₄.UD u AN
8 šá ŠÚ-ú NU IGI ⌈x x x⌉ [
lower edge blank

rev.
1 ITI.BI 15 N[A ... KUR]
2 MU.BI SIG 30 <šamáš> G[UB]
3 erasure
4 erasure
5 ZALÁG(?) x x AN.KU₁₀ sin u AN.KU₁₀ šamáš
5a uninscribed   UD 1 KÙŠ UD 1 (?)
6 [ina] É ni-ṣir-tú šá MÚL.BABBAR
7 [LÚ] ⌈a⌉-lid
8 [   ]x uninscribed
lower edge uninscribed

Critical Apparatus:

obv. 4: Note that LÚ.TUR is abbreviated to LÚ. See also rev. 7, and Text 14:5.
obv. 8: For the last several signs only the tops of wedges are visible. One expects KI *šamáš* *šú-nu* "they were with the sun."
rev. 2: *šamáš* (20) appears to be omitted from the standard expression ITI.MN n *šamáš* GUB "solstice was on the nth of MN." Perhaps because the date was the thirtieth, the additional two Winkelhaken were inadvertently left off, or perhaps GUB alone sufficed.
rev. 5a: Signs are smaller than the rest of the text, as though a gloss.
rev. 8: Just after the break all that is visible is the tail of a horizontal wedge.

TEXT 13 BM 47642

Translation

obv.
1 Year 88, Seleucus was king.
2 [Ab]u 30, night of the 4th, beginning of night, the moon was
3 below the bright star of the Furrow (= α Virginis) by 1 5/6 cubits,
   the moon passed 1/2 cubit
4 to the east. On the 4th day the child was born.
5 In his hour, the moon was in Libra,
6 sun in Leo, Jupiter and Saturn
7 in Scorpius, Venus in Gemini, Mercury and Mars
8 which had set were not visible, [they were with the sun.]
rev.
1 That month, moonset af[ter sunrise] was on the 15th, [the last
   lunar visibility occurred on the ...]
2 That year, (summer) solstice was on the 30th of Simanu
3 erased
4 erased
5 .... eclipse of moon and sun.
5a   .... (?)
6 [In] the *bīt niṣirti* of Jupiter
7 [the child] was born.
8 [...]

Commentary:

obv.2-4: The position of the moon is given relative to the normal star "Bright
star of the Furrow" (= α Virginis), which had a longitude of 172.97° (+6.16°
= 179.13°) on this date. The computed longitude for the moon on this date is
179.74° (see table below).
rev.5: The reference to solar and lunar eclipses is in broken context. It is
difficult to account for their mention here, because in the year of this birth, no
eclipses were visible.

Astronomical Data:

	λ Text	λComputed (-223 July 29*)		
moon	Libra	179.74°	=	Libra 0°
sun	Leo	127.95°	=	Leo 8°
Jupiter	Scorpius	226.64°	=	Scorpius 17°
Venus	Gemini	82.89°	=	Gemini 23°
Mercury	(with the sun)	121.14°	=	Leo 1°
Saturn	Scorpius	220.41°	=	Scorpius 10°
Mars	(with the sun)	122.53°	=	Leo 3°

*Computed for 18.00 UT, or shortly after sunset in Babylon. The computed longitudes reflect
a +6.16° adjustment for -223.

Text 14 BM 36620

Text 14 (BM 36620 = 80-6-17,350 [L*1464])

92 S.E. VII. 12(?) = -219 Oct. 21
Previously unpublished

Transcription

obv.
upper edge
   ina a-mat ᵈEN u GA[ŠAN-ía liš-lim]
1 MU.1,32.⌜K⌝[AM ¹An LUGAL]
2 ITI.DU₆ 30 GE₆ 1[2(?) ina SAG GE₆ sin]
3 SIG MÚL ár šá SAG HUN
4 sin 1/2 KÙŠ ana NIM DIB U₄(?).[...]

5 LÚ a-lid ina si-ma-ni-[šú sin ina HUN(?)]
6 šamáš ina GÍR.TAB MÚL.BABBAR [ina HUN]
7 dele-bat u GENNA i[na(?) PA(?)]
8 GU₄.UD u AN [šá ŠÚ-ú NU IGI.MEŠ]
9 KI šamáš šú-nu [ITI.BI(?)]
rev.
1 14 NA 2[7 KUR]
2 ITI.GAN 20 [šamáš GUB]
3 ITI.ŠE GE₆ 1[4 AN.KU₁₀ sin]
4 ina RÍN TIL-tim GAR-a[n]
5 U₄.28 AN.[KU₁₀ šamáš]
6 ina HUN BAR DIB [ ]
ca. 2 lines to bottom of rev., uninscribed.

Critical Apparatus

line obv. 5: Note that *šerru* is written LÚ, as in Text 13:4.
rev. 1: The date of the last lunar visibility before sunrise is restored by means of the almanac text LBAT *1118+ *1119 (=BM 40101+ 55536):17.
rev. 2: The date of winter solstice is resolved by the Uruk Scheme.
rev.3: The date of the lunar eclipse has been restored by means of modern computation. See commentary below.

Translation

u.e.
By the command of Bēl and B[ēltīja may it go well].
obv.

1 Year 92 [(S.E.), Antiochus (III) was king.]
2 Tašrītu 30, night of the 1[2th(?), first part of night, the moon was]
3 below "the rear star of the head of the Hired Man (= α Arietis).
4 The moon passed 1/2 cubit to the east (of α Arietis) ..[..]
5 the child was born, in [his] hour, [the moon was in Aries(?),]
6 the sun was in Scorpius, Jupiter [was in Aries],
7 Venus and Saturn (were) i[n Sagittarius],
8 Mercury and Mars [which had set were not visible.]
9 They were with the sun. [That month(?),]
rev.
1 moonset after sunrise was on the 14th, [last lunar visibility
        before sunrise on the] 2[7th.]
2 [Winter solstice (was)] on the 20th of Kislīmu.
3 Addaru, night of the 1[4th a lunar eclipse,]
4 Totality occurr[ed] in Libra.

5 On the 28th day an ecl[ipse of the sun]
6 in Aries, one-half month having passed (since the previous eclipse).

Commentary

obv.2: The date of the horoscope is restored with the help of modern
computation within the requirements of the preserved textual data, namely
that Mercury and Mars must be sufficiently close to the sun to have reached
last visibility in the west, the sun must be in Scorpius, and Venus and Saturn
must be in the same zodiacal sign. Jupiter's longitude is broken and the moon
can only be used to approximate the time once a date has been obtained.
Within the possible dates derived from the planetary longitudes, the best
correlations fall at Oct. 20/21 and from there the longitude of the moon near
α Arietis (corresponding to 5.67° in -300 and 9.82° in 0 according to the table
in Sachs-Hunger, *Diaries*, p.17, or 8.17° in -219) fits quite well with the 12th
day of *Tašrītu*. The astronomical computations are given so as to correlate
with the time of birth soon after moonset toward morning of Oct.21,, so
Oct.21 is used as the Julian equivalent (rather than Oct.20 which is the day on
which sunset marking the beginning of the Babylonian day occurred). See
table of astronomical data below.
obv. 5-7: Zodiacal signs have been restored on the basis of the modern data, as
in the table below. Ancient support comes from an almanac text LBAT *1118
+ *1119 (BM 40101 + 55536) which preserves data for this year and month.
Referring to Jupiter, the almanac records its opposition to the sun on the 23rd
as well as its position in Aries (BM 40101+ obv. 14). Venus is stated as having
reached Sagittarius on the 10th (BM 40101+ obv. 16).
obv. 8: The rising and setting times of the sun, Mercury, and Mars were used
to check the dating of the text. On the presumed date of the birth, the sun,
Mercury and Mars all set within one hour of one another, which is agrees
satisfactorily with the statement in the text that the two planets were "with the
sun" and had "set," i.e., had had their last appearances in the west.
rev. 1: The date of the last lunar visibility is given in the almanac LBAT
*1118+ (BM 40101+) obv. 17: 27 KUR.
rev. 2: Date of winter solstice is in accordance with the Uruk Scheme, cycle 4
year 17 (see HAMA p.362 Table 3).
rev.3-4: The lunar eclipse is also reported in the almanac LBAT *1118+ (BM
40101+) rev. 10: GE$_6$ *ana* ZALÁG AN.KU$_{10}$ sin ina [x] and corresponds to
that of -218 March 20 (=S.E.92 Addaru 14). This eclipse began around 1:00
AM in Babylon (first contact was 23.02 UT and last contact 2.45 UT). The
lunar longitude at maximum phase (175°, adjusted +6°=181° or Libra 1') agrees
very well with the text.
rev.5-6: The solar eclipse is to have occurred one-half month after the lunar
eclipse. For the terminology BAR DIB "1/2 (month) passed," see LBAT
1427:9'; 1249 rev. 8'; and 320:10'. This situation can apply to either a solar or

a lunar eclipse, but must refer to an eclipse of one kind followed by 1/2 month an eclipse of the other kind. No two lunar eclipses or solar eclipses can be separated by 1/2 month. Computation shows that no solar eclipse occurred 1/2 month after the lunar eclipse recorded in rev. 3f.

Astronomical Data

	λ Text		λ Modern (Oct. 21 -219*)
moon	[Aries]	7.88	= Aries 8°
sun	Scorpius	210.5	= Scorpius 0°
Jupiter	[Aries]	9.02	= Aries 9°
Venus	[Sagittarius]	246.59	= Sagittarius 7°
Saturn	[Sagittarius]	267.29	= Sagittarius 27°
Mercury	(with sun)	227.08	= Scorpius 17°
Mars	(with sun)	202.75	= Libra 23°

Computed for 3.00 UT, or just before sunrise Babylonian local time, adjusted +6.1° for -219.

Text 15 BM 36796

TEXT 15 (BM 36796 = 80-6-17,534 [L*1466])

S.E. 109 XI.9 = -201 Feb.4
Previous publication: F. Rochberg, *OrNS* 58 (1989), p.114-117.

Transcription

obv.
1 MU.1,49!.KAM ^{I}An u ^{I}An A-šú LUGAL.MEŠ
2 ITI.ZÍZ 30 GE$_6$ 9 SAG GE$_6$
3 sin ina IGI ŠUR ULÙ 1 KÙŠ
4 GE$_6$ 9 USÁN LÚ.TUR GUD(?) ⌜x x⌝
5 ina si-ma-ni-šú sin ina TIL MÚL.MÚL
6 šamáš ina GU MÚL.BABBAR ina ⌜RÍN(?)⌝
7 dele-bat šá ŠÚ-ú NU IGI KI
8 šamáš šu-ú GU$_4$.UD ina GU
9 GENNA ina A AN ina MÁŠ

rev.
1 ITI.BI 14 NA 28 KUR
2 MU.BI GAN 28 šamáš GUB
3 ina É ni-ṣir-tu$_4$
4 šá MÚL.BABBAR LÚ.TUR MÍ(?) ⌜x x⌝.MEŠ(?)
remainder uninscribed

Critical Apparatus

obv. 1: Text has year 1,59 for 1,49.
obv. 3: The normal star name ŠUR ULÙ (= ζ Tauri) is abbreviated from ŠUR GIGIR *ša* ULÙ "the southern .... of the Chariot."
obv. 4: Following LÚ.TUR are three imperfectly preserved signs that appear to be GUD ŠUB.MEŠ/ or -ú. We expect some form of *alādu* "to be born," or even *rehû* "to be conceived."
rev. 4: Following LÚ.TUR there seems to be a clear MÍ, i.e., a daughter. The verb is apparently the same as in obv.4.

Translation

obv.
1 Year 109 (S.E.), Antiochus (III) and Antiochus his son, were
      the kings.
2 Month Šabaṭu 30, night of the 9th, beginning of night.
3 The moon was 1 cubit west of the southern .... (of the Chariot, = ζ Tauri).

4 Night of the 9th, evening watch, the child ....
5 in his hour (of birth), the moon was at the end of Taurus,
6 sun was in Aquarius, Jupiter was in Libra,
7 Venus which had set was not visible, it was with
8 the sun; Mercury was in Aquarius,
9 Saturn in Leo, Mars in Capricorn.
rev.
1 That month, moonset after sunrise on the 14th; last lunar
    visibility before sunrise on the 28th.
2 That year, the 28th of Kislīmu was the (winter) solstice.
3 In the *bīt niṣirti*
4 of Jupiter, the daughter .....

Commentary

obv.3: The normal star ζ Tauri had longitude 54.19° ($+5.85° = 60.04°$), which
agrees well with the zodiacal position given in line 5 as *ina* TIL MÚL.MÚL
"the end of Taurus."
obv. 7-9: A diary for S.E.109 is preserved for the end of the month of our
horoscope. Relevant to the horoscope is the planetary summary given in diary
No.-202 rev.4' (see Sachs-Hunger, *Diaries*, p.212) where it closely parallels the
data in the horoscope: [... *dele-bat]* ina ŠÚ *ina* TIL GU IGI *ina* 20+[x]
G[U₄.UD *ina* NI]M *ina* TIL GU ŠÚ(?) GENNA *ina* A AN *ina* MÁŠ [...] "[...
Venus'] first appearance in the west in the end of Aquarius; around the
20+[xth, Mercury's] last' appearance [in the ea]st in the end of Aquarius;
Saturn was in Leo; Mars was in Capricorn [...]".
obv.9: A goal-year text for S.E. 168 (LBAT 1265) contains data for Saturn
extracted from a diary one synodic period (59 years) preceding the goal year,
hence corresponding to the date of the horoscope, S.E. 109. In the portion of
the goal year text relevant to month XI, the planet Saturn is said to be 1 1/2
KÙŠ *ina* IGI GIŠ.KUN A "1 1/2 cubits to the west of the Rump of the Lion
(= θ Leonis)" (LBAT 1265:18'). Agreement is found with the horoscope which
assigns Saturn the zodiacal sign Leo, and cf. diary No.-202 rev.4' for Saturn in
Leo.
rev.2: The winter solstice date is in accordance with the Uruk Scheme.

Astronomical Data

        The birth occurred during the evening watch of *Šabaṭu* 9. The
corresponding Julian date must be Feb.4, corresponding to the appropriate
portion of the Babylonian day, i.e., sometime shortly after sunset.

	λ *Text*	λ *Computed (-201 Feb. 4*)*		
moon	end of Taurus	56.68	=	Taurus 27°
sun	Aquarius	318.29	=	Aquarius 18°
Jupiter	end of Leo	181.92	=	Libra 2°
Venus	(with the sun)	325.62	=	Aquarius 26°
Mercury	Aquarius	291.38	=	Capricorn 21°
Saturn	Leo	134.17	=	Leo 14°
Mars	Capricorn	291.53	=	Capricorn 22°

*Computed for 16.00 UT, which was about one hour after sunset in Babylon (sunset was 14.58 UT on this day). Longitudes are adjusted by +5.85° for -201.

TEXT 16 (W.20030/10)

Horoscope (b, obv.) S.E. 113 VII.14 = -198 Oct.31
Horoscope (a, rev.) S.E. 112 III.3 = -199 June 5
copy: Baghdader Mitteilungen Beiheft 2 pl.35 Nr. 81

Transcription

obv.(?)
1 MU.1.ME.13 ⌜DU$_6$⌝ GE$_6$ 14 LÚ.TUR a-lid
2 U$_4$.BI šamáš ina GÍR.TAB
3 sin ina MÚL
4 MÚL.BABBAR ina 10 MÁŠ ⌜ina ZALÁG(?) x x⌝
5 dele-bat ina 4 MÁŠ ⌜ina ZALÁG x x⌝
6 GU$_4$ ina 8 GÍR.TAB KI šamáš
7 GENNA ina 3 RÍN GUB-zu
8 AN ina 10 PA
9 sin TA SIG x(?) pa-nu-šú ana MURUB$_4$ GAR.MEŠ
10 sa-ba-tu$_4$ x U$_4$.ME(?) ⌜SIG$_5$⌝ IGI

rev.(?)
1 SIG GE$_6$ 3 ina ZALÁG i-x-⌜x⌝
2 LÚ.TUR a-lid U$_4$.BI šamáš ina ⌜MAŠ.⌝MAŠ
3 30 ina 15 ALLA
4 MÚL.BABBAR ina 26 GÍR.TAB ina ZALÁG ⌜x x⌝
5 dele-bat U$_4$.BI ina KUR ina 5 MAŠ IGI SIG$_5$
6 GU$_4$ ina 27(?) MAŠ.MAŠ KUR!?-ád
7 GENNA ina 10 ABSIN NU GUB
8 AN ina 10 MÚL GUB
9 BE-ma ZI sin [x] (erasure) SIG$_5$
10 30 TA LAL ana MURUB$_4$ pa-nu-šú GAR.MEŠ

Critical Apparatus

The sequence of the dates of the two horoscopes suggests that obverse and
reverse of the tablet be reversed from that indicated by the copy. Against this,
however, is the fact that the beginning of reverse line 1, in not giving the year
number would be unusually abbreviated if indeed it were the first line of the
tablet.
rev. 5 This line is uncertain. For one thing, Venus' longitude appears to be 50
rather than 5 in the copy. Also, Gemini is abbreviated to MAŠ in this line, but
written MAŠ.MAŠ in rev.6. Text needs collation. Following MAŠ.MAŠ, the
copy appears to be UR$_5$.

Translation

obv.

1 Year 113 (S.E.) Tašrītu, night of the 14th, the child was
   born.
2 That day, the sun was in Scorpius,
3 the moon was in Taurus.
4 Jupiter was in 10° Capricorn, last part of the night ....
5 Venus in 4° Capricorn, last part of the night ....
6 Mercury in 8° Scorpius with the sun,
7 Saturn in 30° Libra, present,
8 Mars in 10° Sagittarius.
9 The moon goes from (extreme) negative latitude toward the node.
10 .... he will see good fortune (lit.: propitious days).

rev.

1 Simanu, night of the 3rd, last part of night ...
2 the child was born. That day, the sun was in Gemini,
3 the moon was in 15° Cancer,
4 Jupiter in 26° Scorpius, the last part of the night ...
5 Venus' first visibility that day in the east in 5° Gemini, favorable(?).
6 Mercury reached(?) 27° Gemini.
7 Saturn in 10° Virgo, not present.
8 Mars in 10° Taurus, present.
9 If the progress of the moon .... favorable.
10 The moon goes from (extreme) positive latitude toward the node.

Horoscope (obv.) Commentary

obv.7: GUB= *uzuzzu* "to stand," or "be present," often said of planets in
eclipse omens or reports for those planets visible during an eclipse (especially
solar), for example, (If the moon is eclipsed in Leo ... and) ᵈSAG.ME.GAR NU
GUB-*iz* "Jupiter is not present," JNES 43 134:5', also ibid. 16', rev. 19; *ina*
AN.KU₁₀-*šú dele-bat* GENNA *u* MUL.KAK.SI.SÁ GUB-*u'* ÍB.TAK₄ ᵈUDU.
IDIM.MEŠ NU GUB.MEŠ "in his eclipse Venus, Saturn, and Sirius were
present, the rest of the planets were not present" LBAT 1448 rev.3-4 (lunar
eclipse report), also LBAT 1438 rev.3; LBAT 1442 rev.6.
    In this horoscope, computation shows that Saturn was above the horizon
just before sunrise, altitude 32.08 at 3.00 UT = 6:00 AM Babylonian local time.
Cf. the same terminology in rev.7-8.
obv.9: *sin* TA SIG x *pa-nu-šú ana* MURUB₄ GAR.MEŠ literally, "the moon
sets its face from below toward the middle." The term NIM *u* SIG, "high and
low," or "above and below" is known from astronomical texts as a technical

term for lunar latitude. See ACT 200 obv. I 20, and discussion in A. Aaboe
and J. Henderson, "The Babylonian Theory of Lunar Latitude and Eclipses
According to System A," *Archives Internationales d'Histoire des Sciences* 25
(1975), pp.181-122; also CAD s.v. *šapālu*. The reference point is the ecliptic,
with the moon either above or below it. The points of reference for the lunar
latitude statements are the lunar nodes, the two points where the moon's path
crosses the ecliptic, and the nodal zone seems to be designated by the "middle"
(MURUB$_4$). The moon can be in relation to the nodes as follows: 1)
approaching the ascending node, going with negative latitude, increasing
toward 0, 2) passing the ascending node, going with increasing positive latitude,
3) approaching the descending node, going with decreasing positive latitude, or
4) passing the descending node, going with negative latitude, decreasing toward
the maximum negative of -5°. In Babylonian ephemerides, these four
possibilities are expressed with the terms LAL and U, designated 1) LAL LAL
"positive increasing" 2) LAL U "positive decreasing" 3) U U "negative
decreasing" and 4) U LAL "negative increasing."   The other horoscope
containing a reference to lunar latitude is Text 10, also from Uruk, and
discussed by Sachs in JCS 6, p.61 in the commentary to lines 3-4.   In the
present horoscope, the statement in obv.9 has the moon going from the point
of extreme negative latitude (SIG) to the nodal zone (*ana qablīti* "the middle").
This would seem to describe progress toward the nodal zone from "below,"
i.e., with negative latitude increasing toward 0° (ascending node). I would
translate this as decreasing negative latitude. (Fig. a)

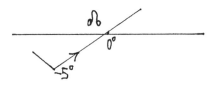

However, computation for this date shows the moon moving away from the
node, approaching the maximum negative latitude of -5°, i.e., moving with
increasing negative latitude. Computed latitudes for the moon on this date for
the hours before the time of the text show

> *Time UT Lunar Latitude*
> 1   -4.92
> 2   -4.93
> 3   -4.94 (this was just before sunrise)

clearly indicating progress toward maximum negative latitude, not toward the
node. (Fig.a') Cf. Commentary to rev. 10.

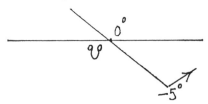

Horoscope b (obv.) Astronomical Data

The horoscope does not state the time of birth in the introductory lines where one would expect to find it, but in the planetary data. There several indications that the birth was in the last part of the night, before sunrise. These are 1) the phrase "*ina* ZALÁG" found at the end of obv. 4 and 5, and 2) the statement that Saturn was "present." In order for Saturn to be visible, the time must have been toward morning, as Saturn's altitude before sunrise was 32.08 as opposed to -39.29 in the evening.

	λ Text	λ Computed (-198 Oct.31*)
moon	Taurus	47.8 = Taurus 18°
sun	Scorpius	220.25 = Scorpius 10°
Jupiter	Capricorn 10°	275.29 = Capricorn 5°
Venus	Capricorn 4°	267.39 = Sagittarius 27°
Mercury	Scorpius 8°	227.67 = Scorpius 18°
Saturn	Libra 3°	183.11 = Libra 3°
Mars	Sagittarius 10°	248 = Sagittarius 8°

---

* Computed for 3.00 UT = 6:00 AM Babylonian local time (midnight epoch), and adjusted +5.81° for the year -198.

Horoscope (a) rev. Commentary

rev. 7: Following the position of Saturn is the comment NU GUB "not present." Computation indicates a negative altitude for Saturn at the time of birth, shortly before sunrise.

rev. 8: A similar comment is given following the Mars position, GUB "present." Computation confirms positive altitude (23.29), enough that the planet would have been visible at the time of the birth.

rev. 9: The term ZI, "progress," from *nasāhu* "move forward," is interpreted as such on the basis of the use of this term in the ephemerides. ZI as "velocity," or progress in longitude is common in ACT lunar procedure texts. See ACT glossary.

rev.10: A lunar latitude statement, saying *sin* TA LAL *ana* MURUB₄ *pa-nu-šú* GAR.MEŠ literally, "the moon sets its face from above toward the middle." This seems to describe progress toward the nodal zone from "above," i.e., from positive latitude to the descending node, or movement with decreasing positive latitude. (Fig. b)

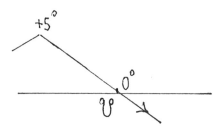

Computed latitudes here show

Time UT	Lunar Latitude
1	-4.19
1.75	-4.17
3	-4.14

indicating progress toward 0° (ascending node). (Fig.b', as in Fig. a)

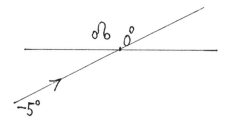

Horoscope (rev.) Astronomical Data

	λ Text	λ Computed (-199 June 5*)		
moon	Cancer 15°	118.61	=	Cancer 29°
sun	Gemini	75.45	=	Gemini 15°
Jupiter	Scorpius 26°	237.85	=	Scorpius 28°
Venus	Gemini 5°	62.37	=	Gemini 2°
Mercury	Gemini 27°	84.4	=	Gemini 24°
Saturn	Virgo 10°	157.23	=	Virgo 7°
Mars	Taurus 10°	38.28	=	Taurus 8°

---

* Computed for 1.75 UT = 4:45 AM Babylonian local time (midnight epoch), and adjusted +5.83° for the date of the text.

TEXT 17 BM 41054 =81,4,28,601

Date: S.E. 136 VII.[19?] = -175 Oct. 20
Previously unpublished

Transcription

obv.
1 [MU.1.ME]⌜36⌝.KAM [I]Se-lu-ku LUGAL ITI.DU_6 1 [GE_6 19(?)]
x sin ina MAŠ.MAŠ (written around edge to rev.1)
2 MÚL.BABBAR ina GÍR.TAB dele-bat u GU_4.UD ⌜ina?⌝ [ITI.BI(?)]
3 ⌜x⌝ 27 KUR GAN 21 šamáš GUB
3a [ ]DIŠ AN BAR KI ni 5(?) [...]
4 [ ] x [
remainder broken

rev.
1 [ ] blank [
2 [ ] x ABSIN(?) ITI.BAR U_4(?).x[
3 [DU]MU.SAL šá [f]Ta-pu-ú-[d]EN
Critical Apparatus
obv. 3a: Signs are written small, as though a gloss, but to what? Readings are uncertain for lack of context.
rev. 2 Following ITI.BAR, the sign looks possibly like PA.

Translation

obv.
1 [Year 13]6 Seleucus (IV) the king, Tašrītu 1, [night of the
19th(?)] moon in Gemini
2 Jupiter in Scorpius, Venus and Mercury in(?) [...]
3 [...] on the 27th last lunar visibility before sunrise, (winter)
solstice was on Kislīmu 21.
3a ....
4 ....
remainder broken

rev.
1 [...] blank [...]
2 [...] .... Nisannu, the [...]th day [...]
3 [da]ughter of [f]Tappu-Bēli(?) [...]

TEXT 17 BM 41054

Commentary

obv. 2: It seems that Venus and Mercury should at least be in the same sign, since it is common for planets in the same sign to be listed consecutively. Computation for the date suggested by other evidence in this text, however, does not confirm Venus and Mercury in the same sign. See astronomical data below.

obv. 3: The date of winter solstice, which ordinarily can provide a reliable limiting factor for dating a text within the period in which the Uruk Scheme was used, is problematic here. A *Kislīmu* 21, which is clearly written in the text, does not occur in the Uruk Scheme. If -175 is correct for this horoscope, *Kislīmu* 27 is expected.

Dating

Several bits of evidence provided limits on the date for this horoscope. The only clearly attested planetary longitude was that for Jupiter. The regnal year is partly broken, but at least could be limited to a Seleucus. Enough space left in the break at the beginning of the first line suggests MU.1.ME in the break and a partially preserved x.KAM, representing the number beyond 100 of the Seleucid Era year number. The number-sign is damaged, but appears to end in either 5 or 6. This further limits the date to Seleucus IV-VI. In addition, the seventh month (*Tašrītu*) is preserved. Within the span of years from Seleucus IV to VI, Jupiter was in Scorpius in the month of *Tašrītu* (October) in only two years, -186 and -175, both years during the reign of Seleucus IV. In year -186, Jupiter was passing out of Scorpius into Sagittarius at the beginning of *Tašrītu*. By process of elimination then, I have proposed -175 as the year of the horoscope. Given the fragmentary nature of the text, this dating must be considered uncertain and provisional, as the astronomical data does not confirm the positions of Venus and Mercury in the same sign.

Astronomical Data

	λ Text	λ Computed (-175 October 20*)		
moon	Gemini	73.64	=	Gemini 14°
sun	[ ]	209.73	=	Libra 30° (or Scorpius 0°)
Jupiter	Scorpius	253.5	=	Scorpius 13.5°
Venus	[ ]	175.73	=	Virgo 26°
Mercury	[ ]	202.73	=	Libra 23°
Saturn	[ ]	104.37	=	Cancer 14°
Mars	[ ]	317.06	=	Aquarius 17°

---

* Computed for 16 UT = 7:00 PM Babylonian local time (midnight epoch), and adjusted +5.49 for the year in question.

TEXT 18 BM 35516

TEXT 18 (BM 35516)

S.E. 169 XII.6 =-141 March 1
Previous publication: Epping (and Strassmaier), *ZA* 4 (1889), pp.168-171;
Kugler, *SSB* II pp.554-558; Sachs, *JCS* 6, pp.62-63
photo: *JCS* 6, pl.IV.
copy: Strassmaier, *ZA* 3 (1888), 149f.

Transcription

obv.
1 [MU.1.M]E 1,9.KAM ᶦDi-mit-ri [LUGAL(?)]
2 ITI.ŠE 30 GE₆ 6 SAG GE₆ sin
3 ina IGI ŠUR GIGIR šá SI 1 KÙŠ
4 6 ina ZALÁG LÚ.TUR a-lid
5 ina si-man-ni-šú sin ina SAG MAŠ.MAŠ
6 šamáš ina ZIB.ME MÚL.BABBAR ina RÍN dele-bat
7 u AN ina MÁŠ GENNA ina A
8 ITI.BI 14 NA
Edge
1 27 KUR
rev.
1 MU.1.ME 1,10.K[AM]
2 BAR 4 LÁL-t[im]
3 ina É ni-ṣi[r(?)-tu₄(?)]
4 šá MÚL.BABBAR LÚ.TUR a-lid
remainder of reverse uninscribed

Critical Apparatus

See JCS 6, pp.62-63.

Translation

obv.
1 [Year 1]69 (S.E.), Demetrios (II Nicator) [was king(?).]
2 Addaru 30, night of the 6th, beginning of night, the moon
3 was 1 cubit west of the northern .... of the Chariot (β Tauri),
4 On the 6th in the last part of night, the child was born.
5 In his hour (of birth), the moon was at the beginning of
   Gemini,
6 the sun was in Pisces, Jupiter in Libra, Venus
7 and Mars in Capricorn, Saturn in Leo.
8 That month, moonset after sunrise occurred on the 14th,

edge
1 the last lunar visibility was on the 27th.

rev.
1 Year 170 (S.E.)
2 Nisannu the 4th (was the date of vernal) equinox.
3 In the *bīt niṣi[rti]*
4 of Jupiter, the child was born.
remainder of reverse (probably) uninscribed

Commentary

obv. 2-3: A lunar position with respect to the normal star β Tauri is given for the beginning of the day on which the birth occurred. This underscores the fact that when the normal star position of the moon is given (see Texts 6, 13, and 15), that time is not to be read as equivalent to the time of birth, and indeed, in this case, the moon was invisible at the time of the birth ("in the last part of night"). The normal star statements must simply be direct quotes from diaries. Computation for -141 Feb. 28 15.00 UT (=6:00 PM Babylonian local time) shows the moon with a longitude of 55.31°, agreeing well with the 57.82° of the normal star β Tauri in -141.

rev. 1-2: The date of vernal equinox, S.E.170 Nisannu.4 belongs to the Uruk Scheme, as discussed by Sachs, JCS 6 63 commentary to lines 10-11. It was presumably used in the horoscope because it is in fact nearer to the date of birth than the preceding winter solstice (S.E. 169 Ṭebētu.1), thereby supporting the observation that the dates of whatever cardinal point of the year is closest to the birth was regarded as most astrologically significant.

Astronomical Data

For the lunar longitude of obv. 2f., see commentary. Note that while the text omits the datum on Mercury, the planet was near superior conjunction and therefore was not visible.

	λ Text	λ Modern (-141 Mar.1*)		
moon	beginning of Gemini	63.33°	=	Gemini 3°
sun	Pisces	342.21°	=	Pisces 12°
Jupiter	Libra	202.85°	=	Libra 23°
Venus	Capricorn	295.85°	=	Capricorn 26°
Mercury	omitted	339.14°	=	Pisces 9
Saturn	Leo	145.09°	=	Leo 25°
Mars	Capricorn	283.05°	=	Capricorn 13°

---

*Computed for 4.00 UT, or 7:00 AM Babylonian local time (midnight epoch), and adjusted +5.02° for -141.

TEXT 19 MB 81561

Text 19 (BM 81561 = Bu.91-5-9,1693)

SE 172 [VI].13 = -139 Sept.7
Previously unpublished

Transcription

upper edge [ina a-mat E]N? u? GAŠAN-ía liš-lim
obv.
1 [MU.1.ME].1,12.KAM ᴵAr-šá-ka-a LUGAL
2 [ITI.KI]N 30 GE₆ 13 ⸢x⸣ USÁN(?)
3 ina si-ma-ni-šú sin ⸢x x x⸣
4 [šam]áš ina ABSIN MÚL.BABBAR ina PA dele-bat ina RÍN
5 AN ina MAŠ.MAŠ GU₄.UD u GENNA
6 šá ŠÚ-ú NU IGI.MEŠ KI šamáš šú-nu
7 ITI.BI 14 NA 28 KUR
8 MU.BI DU₆ 2 LÁL-tim
lower edge uninscribed
rev. uninscribed

Critical Apparatus

obv. 2: Signs following "13" are difficult. Hunger suggested the possibility of a personal name and to read TAG₄ instead of USÁN.
obv. 3: Expect ZIB.ME for the moon's position (see astronomical data below), however, the traces of signs do not permit such a reading.
obv. 4: The logogram *šamáš* (20) is barely visible, but required by context.

Translation

upper edge [By the command of B]ēl and Bēltīja, may it go well.
1 [Year 7]2 (S.E.), Arsaces was king.

2 [Ulūlu] 30, night of the 13th .... evening watch,
3 In his hour (of birth), the moon was in [Pisces(?),]
4 sun in Virgo, Jupiter in Sagittarius, Venus in Libra,
5 Mars in Gemini, Mercury and Saturn
6 which had set were not visible. They were with the sun.
7 That month, moonset after sunrise on the 14th, last lunar
   visibility on the 28th.
8 That year, (autumnal) equinox was on the 2nd of Tašrītu.

Commentary

obv. 5: In a normal star almanac, confirmation of the position of Mars is
found for the morning of Ulūlu.15: AN *e* MÚL.IGI *[šá še-pit* MAŠ.MAŠ]
"Mars above the front star of the Twins' feet (= η Geminorum) (LBAT 1038
obv. 25)." The longitude of this normal star in -139 was 68.74°, which concurs
with that of the horoscope (see table of astronomical data below).
obv. 5-6: The same normal star almanac contains the following entry for
Saturn for the date S.E. 172 VI.12: GENNA *ina* TIL ABSIN ŠÚ "Saturn's last
visibility was in the end of Virgo (LBAT 1038 obv.24)." Cf. the horoscope
obv.4 for the position of the sun in Virgo.
obv. 8: The date of autumnal equinox belongs to the Uruk Scheme, cycle 9
year 2.

Dating
     The month has been restored on the basis of the normal star almanac
referred to in the commentary (LBAT 1038). The zodiacal positions all
support the restoration as Ulūlu and the day has been decided on the basis of
the reference to the evening watch. The 13th of Ulūlu falls on the Julian dates
Sept. 7/8, with evening belonging to the 7th. The table below is computed for
Sept.7.

Astronomical Data

	λ Text	λ Computed (-139 Sept.7*)	
moon	[ ]	333.20 =	Pisces 3°
sun	Virgo	166.45 =	Virgo 16°
Jupiter	Sagittarius	258.98 =	Sagittarius 19°
Venus	Libra	197.78 =	Libra 18°
Mercury	(with the sun)	171.37 =	Virgo 21°
Saturn	(with the sun)	177.58 =	Virgo 28°
Mars	Gemini	69.2 =	Gemini 9°

*Computed for 16.00 UT = 7:00 PM Babylonian local time (midnight epoch). The computed
longitudes have been adjusted +5.0° for -139.

TEXT 20 BM 78089

TEXT 20 (BM 78089)

SE 186 V.24 = -125 Aug.16
photo:
copy:

Transcription

obv.
1 ⌜MU.1.ME.22.KAM šá ši-i⌝
2 ⌜MU.1.ME.1,26.KAM⌝ ᴵAr-šá-ka-a LUGAL
3 ITI.NE 30 15 NA
4 GE₆ 24 ina ZALÁG LÚ.TUR a-lid
5 ina si-man-ni-šú sin ina MAŠ.MAŠ
6 šamáš ina A MÚL.BABBAR u GENNA
7 ⌜ina ZIB⌝.ME dele-bat ina A
8 GU₄.UD u AN šá ŠÚ-ú
9 NU IGI.MEŠ erasure
lower edge uninscribed

rev.
1 ITI.BI ⌜20+x⌝ KUR
2 MU.BI ŠU.⌜3⌝ šamáš GUB
3 ITI.KIN 14 AN.KU₁₀ sin ina ZIB.ME
4 BAR DIB 28 AN.KU₁₀ šamáš
5 ina TIL ABSIN 5 SI GAR-an
ca.3 blank lines to bottom of rev.

Critical Apparatus

rev.2: For S.E. 186, in accordance with the Uruk Scheme, and the rule that the equinox or solstice date closest to the birthdate is given, read summer solstice on ŠU.⌜3⌝.
Most of the reverse is left uninscribed.

Translation

1 Year 122 (A.E.), which is
2 Year 186 (S.E.) Arsaces was king.
3 Abu, 30. Moonset after sunrise on the 15th.
4 Night of the 24th in the last part of the night, the child was born.
5 At that time, the moon was in Gemini,
6 sun in Leo, Jupiter and Saturn
7 in Pisces, Venus in Leo,
8 Mercury and Mars which had set
9 were not visible.
rev.
1 That month, last lunar visibility before sunrise was on the
   20+[...]th.
2 That year, (summer) solstice was on Du'ūzu the 3rd.
3 Ulūlu the 14th a lunar eclipse in Pisces.
4 One-half (month) passed by. (Then,) on the 28th, a solar eclipse
5 at the end of Virgo; it made 5 fingers.

Commentary

obv. 6-7: For the zodiacal sign of Saturn, cf. the goal-year text LBAT 1300:16'.
rev. 2: The solstice date is in accordance with the Uruk Scheme, cycle 9 year 16.
rev. 3-4: On the date given for the lunar eclipse (Ulūlu 14 = Sept.4) in fact no eclipse occurred. Huber's program shows the syzygy for the 5th in the morning, rather than the 4th, and indicates that the eclipse was invisibile (only penumbra). The remark in the text that the eclipse "passed by" no doubt reflects this, rather than its referring to an eclipse which occurred in daylight.

The zodiacal sign for the moon on this date seems to be correct in the text. The modern computed lunar longitude of the moon is 338.02° (+4.8° = 342.82°), well into Pisces.

rev. 4-5: The solar eclipse recorded for Ulūlu.28 (=Sept. 18) is confirmed by computation for -125 Sept.19 and was a partial eclipse. The text's zodiacal position for the sun is also confirmed. Solar and lunar longitudes on the 19th at the midpoint of the eclipse (7.19 UT) were 172.64° (+4.8° = 177.44°) and 172.60° (+4.8° = 177.4°) respectively, which are consistent with the text's statement "end of Virgo."

Astronomical Data

	λ Text		λ Computed (-125 Aug.16*)	
moon	Gemini		85.32 =	Gemini 25°
sun	Leo		143.68 =	Leo 24°
Jupiter	Pisces		340.94 =	Pisces 11°
Venus	Leo		133.15 =	Leo 13°
Mercury	(with sun)		142.37 =	Leo 22°
Saturn	Pisces		337 =	Pisces 7°
Mars	(with sun)		152.87 =	Virgo 3°

*Computed for 2.00 UT = 5:00 AM Babylonian local time (midnight epoch). Sunrise was at 2.40 UT and the birth occurred "toward morning." Longitudes are adjusted +4.8° for -125.

TEXT 21 BM 33018

TEXT 21 (BM 33018 = 78-7-30,12 [L*1468])

S.E. 187 VI.22 = -124 Oct. 1
Previous publication: F. Rochberg, *Centaurus* 32 (1989), pp.153-160.

u.e. [ina a-mat ^{d}E]N u ^{d}GAŠAN-ía ⸢liš-lim⸣
obv.
1 [MU.1.M]E.1,27.KAM ^{I}Ar-šá-kam LUGAL
2 ITI.KIN 1 22 ina ZALÁG 24 ALLA
3 U₄ 22 ina 11 si-man LÚ.TUR a-lid
4 ina si-ma-ni-šú sin ina SAG A šamáš ina RÍ[N]
5 MÚL.BABBAR ina HUN dele-bat ina A GENNA ina ZIB.ME
6 AN ina MAŠ.MAS GU₄.UD šá ŠÚ-ú NU IGI
7 ITI.BI 15 NA 17 LÁL-tim
8 27 KUR MU.B[I]
one line blank

rev.
1 [ITI.NE 14.KAM AN.KU₁₀ sin]
2 ina ZIB.ME al-la 2- ⸢ta⸣ [ŠU^{II}.MEŠ]
3 HAB-rat DIR GAR-an
4 28 AN.KU₁₀ šamáš ina ABSIN
5 ki PAP NU IGI
slight space
6 22 ina ZALÁG 24 ALLA!
7 23 ina ZALÁG 9 A

Critical Apparatus:

rev. line 1 The date of the lunar eclipse is restored on the basis of computation. See commentary below.
rev. line 6 ALLA is defective, but context requires it. For a similar formulation, see Text 24 rev.6

Translation

u.e. [By the command of B]ēl and Bēltīja may it go well.
obv.
1 Year 187 (S.E.), Arsaces was king.
2 Ulūlu 1, on the 22nd, last part of night (i.e., toward morning), (the moon was) 24° in
    Cancer
3 day 22 in the 11th hour, the child was born.

4 In his hour (of birth), the moon was in the beginning of Leo, sun was in
   Li[bra],
5 Jupiter in Aries, Venus in Leo, Saturn in Pisces,
6 Mars in Gemini, Mercury, which had set was not visible.
7 That month, moonset after sunrise was on the 15th, (autumnal)
   equinox on the 17th (of Ulūlu).
8 Last lunar visibility before sunrise was on the 27th. That
   year,
rev.
1 [on the 14th of Abu, a lunar eclipse]
2 in Pisces, in excess of [two-thirds]
3 of the disk it (the moon) made.
4 On the 28th (of Abu), an eclipse of the sun in Virgo;
5 when watched for (it) was not observed.
6 On the 22nd before sunrise, (moon) 24° in Cancer,
7 On the 23rd before sunrise, (moon) 9° in Leo.

Commentary

obv. 4: Some discussion of the moon's position with respect to "SAG A" is
required. Two interpretations are possible. One is simply "the beginning of
Leo," a designation of the area within the zodiacal sign, without specification
of the degree of longitude. A number of parallels may be seen in Sachs, JCS
6, e.g., p.57. The expression "TIL + zodiacal sign" is similarly used to designate
the "end" of a sign, or the area from about 18° to the boundary with the next
sign. But in this instance, it is also possible to read the logograms as the name
of the normal star "Head of the Lion," the fixed star ε Leonis. This
interpretation implies the use of normal stars to designate the observed position
of the moon, as is common in diaries. Parallels for the adoption of this practice
in horoscopes can also be found, e.g., Text 4:3-4 or Text 13:3-4 below. In the
present horoscope, the moon was certainly below the horizon at the time of
the birth, which argues against the interpretation of SAG A as ε Leonis (cf.
my previous edition of this text in *Centaurus* 32, pp.153 and 155, where I more
fully considered the normal star position as the likely reading.) Also arguing
in favor of reading "the beginning of Leo" is the terminology *ina* "in" a
zodiacal sign, since the moon cannot be "in" a normal star.
obv. 6: The expression planet *šá* ŠÚ-*ú* NU IGI "the planet which had set was
not visible," here refers to Mercury's last visibility as an evening star (Ω), the
technical term for which is "*ina* ŠÚ ŠÚ," and as can be seen by the longitudes
of Mercury around the date of the birth, the planet was indeed moving
retrograde (see Table on p. 119).
obv. 7: The date of fall equinox is in accordance with the Uruk scheme.

Table for Mercury
(computations for 14.00 UT = 5:00 PM Babylonian local time).
Longitudes have not been adjusted +4.79°.

λ 's for -124 Oct 1	Oct 3
Mercury 198.29	196.42
Sun 185.63	187.64

---

rev. 1-3: The date of the lunar eclipse can be restored by modern computation. A partial eclipse occurred on -124 August 24 (=Abu 14 S.E.187) beginning at 5:00 PM local time and ending around 8:30 local time (corresponding to first contact at 14.06 UT and last contact at 17.46 UT). Sunset on this date was 15.58 UT or about 6:00 PM, so the first phase of the eclipse would not have been visible. The text is correct in assigning the longitude of the moon in eclipse to Pisces. At maximum phase, the moon's longitude for -124 August 24, 15.66 UT was 328.62° (+4.79° = Pisces 3°). This is the point at which the eclipsed moon would just be becoming visible on the eastern horizon. I am grateful for the suggestion of H. Hunger to restore [ŠU^{II}.MEŠ] (*qātāti*) "two-thirds (of the disk)."

rev. 4-5: Independent confirmation of the solar eclipse which was not observed comes from LBAT 448:7', a diary dated to S.E. 186: 28 AN.KU$_{10}$ *šamáš* DIR NU P[AP] "28th day, solar eclipse, cloudy, not observed." The eclipse was not observable because it occurred after sunset. The partial solar eclipse of -124 Sept.7 began at 15.36 UT (=18.36 local time, and note that sunset was 18.38 on that day) and ended at 17.13 UT (=20.32 local time) when the sun was well below the horizon. The horoscope gives the longitude of the sun during the eclipse as Virgo. Computation shows that solar longitude at the onset of the eclipse was 161.91 (+4.79° =Virgo 17°).

rev. 6-7: The interpretation of SAG A in obv. 4 also bears on our understanding of the data given in rev. 6-7, namely the specific longitudes of the moon on the morning of the birth as well as on the morning of the following day. The use of degrees immediately suggests that computation was used to obtain the data, and furthermore, that the purpose of computing these longitudes was to interpolate a position for the moon at the actual time of birth during the 11th seasonal hour. If one makes use of the horoscope's data from rev. 6-7 and interpolates between Cancer 24° (=114°) and Leo 9° (=129°) for the time of birth, the result is 115° at 5:00 PM Babylonian mean time, corresponding to the 11th seasonal hour for a date around fall equinox (the birth was on Oct. 1). To compare this longitude with a Babylonian longitude, we must adjust +4.79°, with the result that the moon was at 120°, or literally, at the "beginning" of Leo.

Dating:

    The data is computed for Oct. 1 since the birth occurred during the 11th seasonal hour, or toward the end of the day. This portion of the Babylonian day (Ulūlu.22) corresponds to Julian Oct. 1, while the beginning of the Babylonian day falls on Sept.30.

Astronomical Data

	λ Text	λ Computed (-124 Oct. 1*)
moon	beginning of Leo	119.76 = Leo 0°
sun	Libra	190.42 = Libra 10°
Jupiter	Aries	16.14 = Aries 16°
Venus	Leo	144.06 = Leo 24°
Saturn	Pisces	347.53 = Pisces 18°
Mars	Gemini	63.25 = Gemini 3°

*Computed for 14.00 UT = 5:00 PM Babylonian local time (midnight epoch), and adjusted +4.79°.

Lunar data in text rev. 6-7:

	λ Text rev.6-7	λ Modern*
moon VI.22 before sunrise Cancer 24°		113.53 = Cancer 24°
moon VI.23 before sunrise Leo 9°		127.69 = Leo 8°

*Computed for -124 Oct. 1 and 2 at 2.00 UT; sunrise was 2.98 UT, and modern longitudes reflect the correction factor +4.79°.

TEXT 22 (BM 41301 = 81-4-28,849)

Horoscope (a) S.E.195 [IV.2]= -116 July 15
Horoscope (b) S.E.197 IV.7 = -114 June 30
Previously unpublished

Transcription

round side (rev.?)
1' [MU 1.ME 1,35.KAM ᴵ]Ar-[šá-kam LUGAL ITI.ŠU 1]
2' [GE₆ 2]ina 7 ⸢si-man⸣ [LÚ].TUR a-li[d ina si-ma-ni-šú sin
    ina]
3' [AB]SIN šamáš ina ALLA MÚL.BABBAR ina GÍR.⸢TAB⸣ d[ele-bat]
4' [ina] ALLA IGI NU PAP MIN GENNA ina⸢ ALLA(?)⸣ A[N(?) ina
    ALLA(?)]
5' [GU₄.U]D šá ŠÚ-ú NU IGI ITI.BI 10+[n NA n KUR]
6' [M]U.BI ITI.SIG 13 šamáš GUB ITI.[N]E
7' [GE₆.2]9 ⸢AN⸣.KU₁₀ šamáš ina ABSIN KI PAP NU IGI I[TI].KIN
8' [GE₆.1]4/15(?) AN.KU₁₀ sin ina HUN TIL-ti[m] ⸢GAR⸣-an

Text 22 BM 41301

9' [MU 1.ME 1,3]7.KAM ᵊAr⌐ LUGAL ITI.ŠU 30
10' [GE₆] 7 ina 6 si-man LÚ.TUR a-lid ina si-ma-ni-[šú]
11' [sin ina] ⌐ALLA⌐ šamáš ina TIL ALLA MÚL.BABBAR ina GU dele-bat ina
  [MAŠ.MAŠ(?)]
12' [GU₄.UD] ina ⌐ALLA?⌐ GENNA u AN šá ŠÚ-ú NU IGI-'u
13' [ITI.ŠU]. ⌐5⌐ šamáš GUB 14 NA 28 KUR
14' [ITI.ZÍ]Z ⌐GE₆⌐.14 AN.KU₁₀ sin
15' [2]8 AN.K⌐U₁₀⌐ šamáš ina A
16' [   ] HAB-rat DIRI GAR-an

17' [   ] 2 KAM(?) u MU x x[...]
lower edge 1 [   ] x DU(?) DIŠ x [...]
lower edge 2 [   ] ⌐a(?)⌐-da-ni(?)[...

other side surface destroyed

Critical Apparatus

  The inscribed side is the rounder side, and the surface of the other side is totally destroyed. The text represents a collection of horoscopes.
rev. (?) 8': The day number at the break is difficult. As traces appear, they favor reading 1]5, however the single vertical just before the 5 is problematic.
rev.(?) 17-lower edge: The text is badly damaged here, but the occurrence of a date, ending with 2.KAM immediately after the break, followed by *u* MU ... "and year ...," points to two dates, possibly corresponding to the dates of the two horoscopes given in the text. These three last lines of the inscribed side of the text may then be a subscript. Such a device would be in keeping with the fact that the tablet presents a collection of horoscopes, perhaps of interest for their dates and/or longitudes. Both contain a lunar and a solar eclipse one-half month apart. Finally, note that both birth dates fall in *Du'ūzu,* within the same part of the day, and have the sun, Mercury, Mars and Saturn all in Cancer (horoscope (a) also has Venus in Cancer):

	Horoscope a	*Horoscope b*
moon	Virgo	Cancer
sun	Cancer	Cancer
Jupiter	Scorpius	Aquarius
Venus	Cancer	[Gemini]
Saturn	Cancer	Cancer
Mars	[Cancer]	Cancer
Mercury	Cancer	Cancer

Translation

rev.(?)
1' [Year 195 (S.E.)] Ar[saces was king, Du'ūzu 1]
2' [night of the 2nd], in the 7th hour the [ch]ild was bo[rn. In
    his hour (of birth) the moon was in]
3' [Vir]go, sun in Cancer, Jupiter in Scorpius ....[Venus
4' [in] Cancer, first visibility, not observed(?), ditto(?), Saturn in Can[cer, Mars
in
    Cancer(?)]
5' [Mercu]ry which had set was not visible. That month [moonset
    after sunrise on the ....th, last lunar visibility before sunrise on the ...]
6' That ye[ar] summer solstice was on the 13th of Simanu, Abu
7' the [29th], an eclipse of sun in Virgo, when watched for was
    not seen. Ulūlu,
8' [night of the 1]4th, an eclipse of moon; totality occurred in Aries

---

9' [Year 19]7 (S.E.), Ar(saces) was king, Du'ūzu 30
10'[night] of the 7th, in the 6th hour the child was born
    in [his] hour (of birth),
11'[the moon was in] Cancer, sun in the end of Cancer,
    Jupiter in Aquarius, Venus in [Gemini(?)]
12'[Mercury] in ⌜Cancer(?)⌝, Saturn and Mars which had set were
    not visible.
13' (Summer) solstice was on the 5th of [Du'ūzu]; moonset after sunrise on the
14th, last
    lunar visibility before sunrise on the 28th.
14'[... Šaba]tu , night of the 14th, an eclipse of the moon.
15'[... (Šabatu,) night of the 2]8th, an eclipse of the sun in Leo,
16'exceeding [... of] the disk.

17'[...] ....[...]
18'[...] .... [...]
19'[...] .... [...]
bottom

Horoscope (a): Commentary

rev.(?) 1: Based on Parker-Duberstein, *Babylonian Chronology*, the lunar month
datum 30/1 has been restored as 1, meaning the Simanu preceding had 30 days.

rev.(?) 2: The day of the month is restored as GE$_6$ 2 on the basis of the best fit
of astronomical data, see table for horoscope (a) below.
rev.(?) 5: Mercury was in superior conjunction with the sun on this date, rising

and setting very close to the times of sunrise and sunset.

rev.(?) 6: The solstice date is in accordance with the Uruk Scheme.

rev.(?) 6-7: The solar eclipse was invisible in Babylon. Oppolzer has an eclipse in -116 Sept. 9, which would correspond precisely to the text's S.E.195 Abu. 29. The longitude of the sun during the eclipse is also in agreement, the text giving Virgo and Oppolzer 163° (tropical longitude) or Virgo 13°.

rev.(?) 7-8: The lunar eclipse corresponds to that of -116 Sept. 24 (=S.E. 195 Ulūlu.14). The day number is broken, so the text cannot be used to confirm. The lunar longitude was 4.05°, or Aries 4°, which is in agreement with the text's Aries. This eclipse was not visible until near totality: moonrise was 14.92 UT, first contact was at 13.44 UT, totality at 15.38 UT, last contact at 17.21 UT. The moon would therefore be seen to rise as an eclipsed moon and remain eclipsed for approximately 2 more hours. Nothing is said about the duration or the time of the eclipse in the horoscope.

Horoscope (a): Astronomical Data

	λ Text	λ Computed (-116 July 15*)	
Moon	Virgo	155.14	= Virgo 5°
Sun	Cancer	113.71	= Cancer 24°
Jupiter	Scorpius	234.08	= Scorpius 24°
Venus	Cancer	110.29	= Cancer 20°
Saturn	Cancer	97.52	= Cancer 8°
Mars	[Cancer]	92.25	= Cancer 2°
Mercury	(with the sun)	122.07	= Leo 2°

*Computed for 10.00 UT, corresponding to the 7th seasonal hour, or about 1:00 PM, Babylonian local time, when daylight lasted 14 hours. Modern computed longitudes have been adjusted by the factor +4.68°.

Horoscope (b): Commentary

rev.(?) 9: Month *Du'ūzu* 30 is confirmed by Parker-Dubberstein, *Babylonian Chronology.*

rev.(?) 13: The summer solstice date may be restored as Du'ūzu.5 according to the Uruk Scheme.

rev.(?) 14: The lunar eclipse is identifiable with that of -113 Jan. 29, occurring shortly after 5 AM and ending just before 9 AM Babylonian local time (from 2.49 to 5.84 UT). The moon set just before 7 AM, so the second half of the eclipse (3rd and 4th contacts) was below the horizon. The moon was in Leo 11° (lunar longitude was 130.63°) at the midpoint of the eclipse.

rev.(?) 15: The solar eclipse is problematic. While a solar eclipse for -113 Feb.12, one-half month from the preceding lunar eclipse is found in Oppolzer (Nr.2601), it was not visible in Babylon. Furthermore, the text indicates that the sun was in Leo, but it was in the diametrically opposite sign Aquarius (solar longitude 325.64°).   Perhaps there was an error produced by the lunar longitude of the preceding eclipse, which was in Leo.

Horoscope (b): Astronomical Data

	λ Text	λ	Computed (-114 June 30*)
moon	Cancer	215.91	=	Scorpius 6°
sun	end of Cancer	98.71	=	Cancer 9°
Jupiter	Aquarius	311.2	=	Aquarius 11°
Venus	[ ]	60.38	=	Gemini 1°
Mercury	Cancer	121.4	=	Leo 1°
Saturn	(with the sun)	119.43	=	Cancer 29°
Mars	(with the sun)	94.43	=	Cancer 4°

---

*Computed for 8.00 UT, corresponding to the 6th seasonal hour, or about 11:00 AM Babylonian local time, and adjusted +4.65°.

TEXT 23 BM 34003

TEXT 23 (BM 34003 [LBAT 1470])

S.E. 223 X.9 = -87 Jan.5
Previously unpublished

Transcription

upper edge ina a-mat [ᵈEN u ᵈGAŠAN-iá liš-lim]
1 MU 2.ME 23.KA[M ᴵAr-šá-kam LUGAL]
2 AB 1 GE₆ 9 MURUB₄ G[E₆]
3 LÚ.TUR a-l[id] ʳinaʳ si!-ma-ni-šú sin
4 ina 5 MÚL.MÚL šamáš ina 20 MÁŠ
5 MÚL.BABBAR ina 27 HUN dele-bat ina 1 [ZIB.ME(?)]
6 GU₄.UD ina 26 ʳPA! GENNA ina 20(?) MAŠ.MAŠʳ
7 AN ina 20 A ʳITIʳ.BI 14 NA
8 28 KUR MU.BI GAN 2ʳ8ʳ [šamáš] GUB
9 GE₆ 29 AN.KU₁₀ [šamáš GAR]
10 ina ZIB.ME 5 ITI DIB [ŠE]
11 GE₆ 13 ʳANʳ.[KU₁₀ sin ina ABSIN(?)]
edge [TI]L-tim GAR [...(?)]
rev.
1 x x x
2 x x
3 x trace
4 x
5 x
6 ina [   ]x-su(?)
7 ʳaʳ-lid x x -[lu]m(?) ᴵAr-x-x

Critical Apparatus

Obv. line 6: The longitude of Saturn has been restored on the basis of modern computation.
Rev.: The seven lines of the reverse are very damaged, with traces possibly of a personal name only vaguely outlined in the last line.

Translation

upper edge By the command of [Bēl and Bēltīja may it go well]
1 Year 223 [(S.E.), Arsaces was king.]
2 Month Ṭebētu 1, night of the 9th, middle of nig[ht,]
3 the child was born. At that time, the moon
4 was in 5° Taurus; sun in 20° Capricorn;
5 Jupiter in 27° Aries; Venus in 1° [Pisces(?)]
6 Mercury in 26° Sagittarius; Saturn in ʳ20(?)°ʳ Geminiʳ
7 Mars in 20° Leo. That month moonset after sunrise occurred on

the 14th;
8 last lunar visibility before sunrise on the 28th; That year
      [(winter)] solstice was Kislīmu 28;....
9 Night of the 29th, eclipse [of the sun; ...]
10 in Pisces. 5 months passed(?) [Addaru]
11 night of the 13th, ecli[pse of the moon; in Virgo(?)]
12 totality occurred. [...(?)]
remainder too fragmentary for translation

Commentary

obv. 8: The winter solstice date for the year of the birth is in accordance with the Uruk Scheme.

obv. 9-10: The date given for solar eclipse occurring during the year of the birth is not clear. If the month is Kislīmu, same month as the solstice in the line preceding, then the date of the eclipse was S.E. 223 Kislīmu.29 or -88 Dec. 26. Indeed, if the month name is not given, the usual practice is for the date to refer to the month last named. In this case then, the solstice date was given for Kislīmu and the following date, the solar eclipse on the 29th, should refer to Kislīmu as well. However, according to modern computation, no solar eclipse occurred on this date. Two other possibilities exist, namely, the eclipse of -88 Sept. 29 (=Ulūlu 28, still S.E.223) or -87 Feb. 24 (=Šabaṭu 28, still S.E.223), but the fact that the month name is not given argues strongly against this. The meaning of the expression 5 ITI DIB, literally, "5 months passed by" is not at all clear in this context. It does not work to separate the solar eclipse from a lunar eclipse either before or after, on the presumption that this solar eclipse occurred in Kislīmu.

obv.10-11: The lunar eclipse date is restored on the basis of computation to Addaru 13 (March 11 -87). This eclipse began shortly before sunrise (sunrise was 3.44 UT and the eclipse's first contact was 3.13 UT) and ended at 6.87 UT or close to 10:00 AM Babylonian mean time. This eclipse could not have been visible much beyond perhaps the appearance of the setting moon just becoming eclipsed. Totality, however, occurred when the moon was at 171.84° = Virgo 22°, which we can restore in the text.

Astronomical Data

	λ Text	λ Computed (-87 Jan.6*)		
moon	Taurus 5°	32.94	=	Taurus 3°
sun	Capricorn	288.02	=	Capricorn 18°
Jupiter	Aries 27°	25.9	=	Aries 26°
Venus	Pisces 1°	330.77	=	Pisces 1°
Mercury	Sagittarius 26°	266.39	=	Sagittarius 26°
Saturn	Gemini [20°]	79.39	=	Gemini 19°
Mars	Leo 20°	141.07	=	Leo 21°

*Computed for 21.00 UT, or about midnight Babylonian local time, and longitudes adjusted +4.28°.

TEXT 24 (BM 77265 = SH 83-9-28,16 [L*1471])

SE 229 IX.[27(?)] = -82 Dec.20
Previously unpublished

Transcription

obv.
1 [MU.2.ME.29 ^{I}Ar-šá-kam]
2 [LUGAL] ITI.GAN 1
3 [UD.27(?)] [m]i-šil GE$_6$ LÚ.TUR
4 [a-lid ina s]i-man-šú sin ina PA
5 [šamáš ina P]A MÚL.BABBAR ina GÍR.TAB
6 [U$_4$.n] GU$_4$.UD ina NIM ina PA IGI
7 [GENNA ina] ABSIN AN ina RÍN dele-bat
8 [šá ŠÚ]-⌜ú⌝ NU IGI ITI.⌜BI⌝
9 [U$_4$ .n NA] 27 KUR MU.BI
10 [ITI.MN] GE$_6$.13 AN.KU$_{10}$ sin

rev.
1 [... I]TI BAR DIB 28
2 [AN.KU$_{10}$ šam]áš ina SAG PA
3 [ki PAP NU] IGI
remainder of reverse uninscribed

Critical Apparatus

obv. 8: After the break only the final vertical of a sign (-ú?) is visible.
The lower edge of the obverse is partly broken away, but nothing seems to be missing.
Only three lines have been inscribed on the reverse, with most of it left uninscribed.

Translation

obv.
1 [Yr. 229 (S.E.) Arsaces was]
2 [king.] Kislīmu 1.
3 [On the 27th(?) day], middle of night, the child
4 [was born. In] his [h]our (of birth), the moon was in Sagittarius,
5 [sun in Sag]ittarius, Jupiter in Scorpius,
6 [On the nth day,] Mercury had its first appearance in the east in Sagittarius,
7 [Saturn was in] Virgo, Mars in Libra, Venus

TEXT 24 BM 77625

---

8 [which had se]t was not visible. That month,
9 [moonset after sunrise was on the ...], last lunar visibility
    on the 27th. That year,
10 [Month ...] night of the 13th, a lunar eclipse,
rev.
1 [...] one-half [mon]th passed by, (and) on the 28th,
2 [an eclipse of the s]un in the beginning of Sagittarius,
3 [when watched for it was not] observed.

Commentary

obv. 6: Between the dates in question, namely the 19th to the 21st, Mercury
was in retrogradation.
obv. 10-rev. 3: The eclipses present some problems of identification.

Dating

Since the day of the month is broken, but the month as well as the time of the birth are preserved, a three-day span between -82 Dec.19 and 21 is possible for this horoscope. The table below provides data for the 20th of December. Plus or minus one day deviation affects the sun $\pm 1°$ and the moon $\pm 13°$, keeping both within the sign Sagittarius.

Astronomical Data

	λ Text	λ Computed (-82 Dec.20*)	
moon	Sagittarius	255.59	= Sagittarius 16°
sun	Sagittarius	271.22	= Capricorn 1°
Jupiter	Scorpius	218.46	= Scorpius 8°
Venus	(with the sun)	276.8	= Capricorn 7°
Mercury	Sagittarius	253.3	= Sagittarius 13°
Saturn	Virgo	164.99	= Virgo 15°
Mars	Libra	207.05	= Libra 27°

---

*Computed for 21.00 UT, corresponding to midnight in Babylon. Longitudes are adjusted +4.21°.

TEXT 25 BM 42025

TEXT 25 (BM 42025(=81-6-25,647)(+) BM 42164(=81-6-25,787) [L*1472F.])

S.E. 231 I.14/15(?) = -80 Apr.22-23(?)
Previously unpublished

Transcription

obv.
1 [MU.2.ME].[3]1.KAM ITI.BAR 30
2 [GE₆ 15-16(?)] LÚ.TUR a-lid ina si-man-šú
3 [sin ina GÍ]R.TAB šamáš ina ⌜MÚL.MÚL MÚL⌝.BABBAR
4 [ina P]A dele-bat ina ⌜HUN⌝ [GENN]A ⌜ina AB⌝[SIN?]
5 AN ina M[AŠ.MAŠ GU₄.UD šá ŠÚ]-⌜ú⌝
6 NU IGI I[TI.BI GE₆.14 A]N.KU₁₀
7 sin ina GÍR.TAB [TIL-tim GAR 14]
8 NA 27 ⌜KUR⌝ [MU.BI]
9 ⌜SIG⌝ U₄.21 ⌜šamáš GUB⌝
end of obv.
rev. uninscribed

Critical Apparatus

All edges are preserved and reverse is uninscribed.
obv. 1-2: The S.E. year number and date have been restored on the basis of computation. See commentary below.
obv. 4: The zodiacal signs, while barely preserved, can be made out with the help of the astronomical data. Venus' sign HUN is quite eroded, but confirmed by computation. At the end of the line the DIŠ of [GENN]A (TUR+DIŠ) is visible, as is *ina* AB[SIN], where one can see the beginning of the KI of ABSIN (KI+HAL).

obv. 5: All that can be seen of Mars' sign is the vertical of MAŠ.MAŠ, although hardly visible on the edge of a large pit in the middle of the obverse.

Translation

obv.
1 [Year 2]31 (S.E.) Nisannu, 30
2 [night of the 15/16th(?)] the child was born. In his
    hour (of birth)
3 [the moon was in Sc]orpius, sun in Taurus, Jupiter
4 [in Sag]ittarius, Venus in Aries, Sat[urn in Vi]rgo,
5 Mars in G[emini, Mercury which had se]t
6 was not visible. [That mo]nth [night of the 14th, a lunar
    eclipse;
7 [totality occurred] in Scorpius. [The 14th]
8 moonset after sunrise, 27th last lunar visibility before
    sunrise. [That year]
9 (summer) solstice was the 21st of [Simanu].

Commentary

obv. 6-7: The same lunar eclipse is reported in the eclipse report LBAT 1444 obv. 1-5, and confirms the date of the horoscope to April -80. According to the eclipse report, this eclipse occurred on Nisannu 14 = April 21. Duration was almost 5 hours, from 18.89 UT to 23.00 UT. As given in the horoscope, the eclipse occurred while the moon was in the zodiacal sign Scorpius. The position of the moon is not preserved in the eclipse report. By computation, lunar longitude during maximal phase was 213.09° (at 21 UT), or Scorpius 3°
obv. 7-8: Restoration of the date of NA is derived from LBAT 1444 rev.2: 14 3,30 [NA].
obv.9: Date of summer solstice belongs to the Uruk Scheme.

Dating
    The best correlation between the text and computed longitudes falls around April 22 and 23. By the 24th, the moon is no longer in the sign Scorpius.

Astronomical data

	λ Text	λ Computed (-80 Apr.23)*		
moon	Scorpius	235.06	=	Scorpius 25°
sun	Taurus	34.51	=	Taurus 5°
Jupiter	Sagittarius	256.76	=	Sagittarius 17°
Venus	Aries	15.46	=	Aries 15°
Mercury	(with the sun)	11.11	=	Aries 11°
Saturn	[Virgo]	171.12	=	Virgo 21°
Mars	[Gemini]	66.21	=	Gemini 6°

*Computed for 16.00 UT = 7:00 PM Babylonian local time, with longitudes adjusted +4.18°.

TEXT 26 BM 35515

TEXT 26 (BM 35515 = SP III 21 [⌊*1474])

S.E. 236 V.25 = -75 Sept.4
previous publication: F. Rochberg, *Orientalia* NS 58, pp.117-119, and plate II.

upper edge
1 ina a-mat ᵈEN u ᵈGASAN-ía liš-lim
obv.
1 MU.2.ME.36.KAM ¹Ar-šá-kam LUGAL
2 ITI.NE 1 U₄.25.KAM ina 12
3 si-man LÚ.TUR a-lid ina s[i-m]a-ni-šú
4 sin ina A šamáš ina ABSIN MÚL.BABBAR
5 [u AN] ina MAŠ.MAŠ dele-bat ina RÍN
6 [GU₄.UD]ˀ inaˀ A GENNA ina GÍR.TAB ITI.BI
7 [13 NA]x 21 GU₄.UD ina NIM
8 [ina A IGI] 26 KUR

rev.
1 [MU.BI] ˹SIG˺ 16 šamáš GUB
2 [UD].˹29˺ AN.KU₁₀ šamáš
3 [in]a ALLA šá DIB ITI.ŠU
4 GE₆ 13 AN.KU₁₀ sin
5 ina GU 1 SI GAR-an
6 25 ina ZALÁG 8 A
7 x- x šu(?)-ú blank

8 [   ] blank

Critical Apparatus

rev. 6: The horizontal wedge read as *ina* appears to have another small horizontal above it. At the end of the line, the A sign is problematic.
rev. 7: There are two Winkelhakens at the beginning of the line. The reading *šu-ú* is uncertain; perhaps 1 KÙŠ ?

Translation

l.e. By the command of Bēl and Bēltīja may it go well.
obv.
1 Year 236 (S.E.), Arsaces was king
2 Abu 1, the 25th day, in the 12th
3 hour the child was born; in his hour (of birth),
4 the moon was in Leo, Sun in Virgo, Jupiter
5 [and Mars] in Gemini, Venus in Libra,
6 [Mercury] in Leo, Saturn in Scorpius; That month
7 [moonset after sunrise was on the 13th] .... on the 21st,
      Mercury's [first appearance] in the east
8 [in Leo], last lunar visibility before sunrise
      was on the 26th.
l.e. [   ] uninscribed
rev.
1 [That year], the (summer) solstice was on the 16th of Simanu.
2 On the 29th [day (of Simanu)] a solar eclipse
3 [i]n Cancer which passed by. Du'ūzu,
4 night of the 13th, a lunar eclipse
5 in Aquarius made 1 finger.
6 On the 25th in the last part of night, (the moon was) 8° in Leo.
7 It was ....

Commentary

obv. 4-8: The astronomical data found in obv.4-8 of the horoscope is duplicated in the almanac for the same date, LBAT 1174:10. The planetary longitudes are not in quite the same order, but agree in every case, as do the dates of the lunar phenomena NA and KUR. Mercury's first appearance in the east appears to have been obtained directly from the almanac. For further discussion, see *OrNS* 58 (1989), pp.119-121.
rev.1: The date of summer solstice is in accordance with the Uruk Scheme, cycle 13 year 9.
rev.2-3: The solar eclipse corresponds to the eclipse of -75 July 9 (according to

Parker-Dubberstein =S.E.236 Simanu 28, which means Parker-Dubberstein should be corrected by one day). The horoscope states that this eclipse "passed by." Indeed, it was not visible in Babylon, as the sun was already below the horizon at first contact, which occurred at 16.92 UT (=19.88 local time). Sunset was 19.12 local time. The text indicates the longitude of the sun during the eclipse as Cancer. At maximal phase the sun was in 107.76° (= Cancer 18°).

rev.3-5: The lunar eclipse corresponds to the eclipse of -75 July 24, a partial eclipse which began at 3.62 UT or a little more than an hour after sunrise (sunrise was 2.13 on this date) and ended at 4.66 UT or around 8:00 AM local time. The lunar longitude at maximum phase was 300.82° (= Aquarius 1°), in excellent agreement with the text.

rev.6: A lunar longitude is given when the moon was visible in the predawn sky, although this longitude, giving degrees within the zodiacal sign, surely does not represent an observation. Sunrise on this date (=Sept.4) was 2.65 UT or roughly 5:40 Babylonian local time. The moon's longitude at 5:00 AM local time, was 130.41° or Leo 10°. The text's Leo 8° is in excellent agreement, particularly inasmuch as we cannot know precisely for how much "before sunrise" the Babylonian longitude was computed.

Dating

The revision of the date from Sept. 3 to 4 over the previous publication (*OrNS* 58, p.117) reflects the correlation with the Julian date of the part of the Babylonian day in which the birth occurred. The Babylonian date Abu 25 began with sunset that fell on Julian Sept. 3 and continued to Sept. 4. Since the birth is stated to have occurred in the 12th seasonal hour, roughly the end of daylight, this moment correlates with Sept. 4.

Astronomical Data

	λ Text	λ Computed (Sept.4 -75*)		
moon	Leo	136.69	=	Leo 17°
sun	Virgo	163.07	=	Virgo 13°
Jupiter	Gemini	73.6	=	Gemini 14°
Mars	Gemini	77.2	=	Gemini 17°
Venus	Libra	197.98	=	Libra 18°
Mercury	Leo	145.15	=	Leo 25°
Saturn	Scorpius	229.68	=	Scorpius 20°

*Computed for 16.00 UT or roughly 7:00 PM Babylonian local time, to correspond to the 12th seasonal hour of the day. Longitudes are adjusted +4.11° for -75.

TEXT 27 (BM 38104 = 80-10-12,6 [L*1475])

243 S.E. I.20 =-68 Apr.16
Previous publication: F.Rochberg, *Centaurus* 32 (1989), pp.160-162.

Transcription

obv.
1 MU.2.ME.43.KAM ⌜ITI⌝.BAR
2 U$_4$.20.KAM ina 9 si-man LÚ.TUR a-lid
3 ina si-man-šú sin ina TIL MÁŠ ina 18
4 šamáš ina TIL HUN ina 30 MÚL.BABBAR
5 ina PA ina 24 dele-bat ina MAŠ.MAŠ
6 ina 13 GENNA ina GU ina 15
7 AN ina RÍN ina 14 GU$_4$.UD šá ŠÚ-ú NU IGI
8 ⌜ITI⌝.BAR 1 UD.x [...]
lower edge (perhaps erased)
1 27 x x
rev.
1 14 NA 27 KUR
2 MU.BI ITI.NE 28.KAM?!
3 AN.KU$_{10}$ šamáš ki PAP NU IGI
4 ina TIL A
5 ITI.KIN 13 KI ŠÚ šamáš
6 AN.KU$_{10}$ sin al šal HAB-rat
7 DIRI GAR-an ád È-a
8 ina ZIB.ME
upper edge
1 LÚ.TUR BI SIG$_5$ ⌜x x x⌝
2   SIG$_5$ LAL-u

Critical Apparatus

lower edge: The first broken sign could be ⌜ITI⌝ or a number ⌜ 20+n⌝. The
second sign could be ⌜BI⌝. If we read ⌜ITI.BI⌝, however, we would not expect
anything to come before the "14 NA" of rev. 1, and clearly there are more
traces of wedges.
rev.2: Sign at the end of the line looks like KUR, but would make little sense
in the context.
rev.6: Text has *šamáš* instead of *sin*.

Text 27 BM 38104

Translation

obv.
1 Year 243, Nisannu
2 the 20th, in the 9th hour, the child was born.
3 In his hour (of birth), the moon was at the end of Capricorn in 18°,
4 the sun at the end of Aries in 30°, Jupiter
5 in Sagittarius in 24°, Venus in Gemini
6 in 13°, Saturn in Aquarius in 15°,
7 Mars in Libra in 14°, Mercury which had set was not visible.
8 Nisannu [....]
l.e.
1 27 ...
rev.
1 Moonset after sunrise occurred on the 14th, last lunar
   visibility before sunrise on the 27th.
2 That year Abu the 28th day(?),
3 a solar eclipse when watched for, was not seen
4 in the end of Leo.
5 Ulūlu the 13th at sunset (literally: with the setting of the sun)
6 a lunar eclipse exceeding 1/3 disk
7 occurred; (the moon) was (already) eclipsed when it rose
8 in Pisces.
u.e.
1 That child good fortune ....
2 (his) good fortune will diminish.

Commentary

obv. 8: One could anticipate the date of equinox here, although S.E. 243 belongs to cycle 12 year 16 of the Uruk Scheme in which vernal equinox falls in XII$_2$.12. The text here has Nisannu, which is the month of vernal equinox only in years 7, 15, and 18 of the nineteen-year cycle.

rev. 2-4: The date of the solar eclipse is given as Abu 28 or (-68) Aug. 20. Oppolzer has an eclipse on this date for 12.31 UT (about 3 PM local time) at a longitude of 144° (+5° = 149°), or Leo 29°, which concurs with the text's designation "end of Leo," but the eclipse was not visible in Babylon.

rev. 5-8: The lunar eclipse reported here corresponds to the eclipse of -68 Sep.3. It was a partial eclipse of approximately 3 hours duration, having begun shortly before moonrise (moonrise was 15.08 UT and first contact was 14.81 UT), and finishing at 17.87 UT. The text's statement that the eclipse occurred "near the setting of the sun" seems then to refer to the time of the beginning of the eclipse, and indeed, the moon was already eclipsed when it rose. The longitude given in the text is also correct, as the moon was at 342.85° (= Pisces 13°)

during the maximal phase.

Astronomical Data

The date and computations presented here represents a revision +1 day over that found in the previous publication (*Centaurus* 32, p.160). This is meant to reflect the portion of the Babylonian day corresponding to the 9th seasonal hour in which the birth occurred. The fact that Mercury is said to have set is also confirmed by the computed setting times for the sun and Mercury, which were 15.40 and 14.40 UT respectively. Mercury was near inferior conjunction, having had its last appearance in the west as an evening star.

	λ Text	λ Computed (-68 Apr. 16*)		
moon	Capricorn 18°	297.83	=	Capricorn 28°
sun	Aries 30°	27.54	=	Aries 28°
Jupiter	Sagittarius 24°	261.93	=	Sagittarius 22°
Venus	Gemini 13°	72.72	=	Gemini 14°
Saturn	Aquarius 15°	314.23	=	Aquarius 14
Mars	Libra 14°	189.76	=	Libra 10°
Mercury	(with the sun)	15.07	=	Aries 15°

*Computed for 11.50 UT, the equivalent of the 9th seasonal hour on that date, or approximately 2:30 PM Babylonian local time. Longitudes are adjusted +4.02° for -68.

TEXT 28: (BM 37374)

Date: Uncertain
Previously unpublished

Transcription

obv.?
1' traces
2' ina 30 ⌜x⌝ [...]
3' ⌜x⌝ KÙŠ(?) [...]
4' ⌜UD x x⌝ [...]
remainder broken
rev.?
1 ina MÁŠ dele-bat ina M[ÁŠ(?) ...]
2 GU₄.UD ina NIM ina x[ŠÚ(?)/IGI(?) GENNA(?)]
3 ina LU(?) AN ina x[
4 ⌜(2-3 signs)⌝ ina A [
remainder broken

Critical Apparatus

Only the corner is preserved with part of the bottom edge and the left edge of
the obv.(?), and the top and left edge of the rev.(?) Readings on the obv. are all
uncertain.
rev.(?) 1 One expects the longitude for Jupiter to have preceded this line since
Venus is given next. The reading of Venus' longitude is quite uncertain. The
wedges suggest either MÁŠ or perhaps the begin of ABSIN. For the planetary
longitudes to have been distributed so, however, it seems that the tablet ought
to have contained more than one horoscope.
rev.(?) 2 I have restored Saturn (GENNA) in the break since it belongs
between Mercury and Mars in the standard enumeration of planetary
longitudes.

Translation

obv.(?) Too fragmentary for translation
rev.(?)
1 (from previous line:[...Jupiter]) in Capricorn, Venus in
   Vi[rgo(?)
2 Mercury [appeared for the first/last time(?)] as a morning
   star in ..[.; Saturn(?)]
3 was in Aries; Mars in ....

4 .... ina Leo(?)
remainder broken

Commentary

The restoration of the names of the planets is simply too uncertain for any secure dating of this text. In addition, insufficient data from the planets with shorter synodic periods does not allow us to even narrow down the possibilities beyond the 59-60 years between years in which Saturn and Jupiter would be in the appropriate signs (possibly Aries and Capricorn respectively).

rev.(?) 3 For LU=Aries, see Sachs, JCS 6 p.57 note 25 and Ungnad AfO 14 p.256 note 37.

Text 28 BM 37374

Birth Notes

Text 29 (BM 64148 = 82-9-18,4117)

Year 36 Artaxerxes II = -368 ...

Transcription

obv.
1 ITI.ŠU UD.15 MU.36
2 ᴵAr-tak-šat-su KI KUR šamáš
3 LÚ.TUR a-lid
4 ITI.ŠE UD.3.KAM MU.40
5 se-hi-ir
rev.
blank

Translation

1 Du'ūzu the 15th day, year 36
2 of Artaxerxes (II). At sunrise
3 the child was born.
4 Addaru the 3rd day, year 40
5 he was a young child(?).

Critical Apparatus

obv. 5 The verb ṣehēru in the stative is rendered with the SI sign. I am not aware of parallels to the use of SI for ṢI.

Text 29 BM 64148

Text 30 (BM 33563 = Rm IV 119)

S.E. 19 X.16 = -292 ....
tag; birth note
rounder side

Transcription

1 GE₆ 16 ina ZALÁG
2 ITI.AB.KAM
3 MU.19.KAM* ˡSe-lu-uk LUGAL
4 ˡEN-šú-nu A
5 ⌜ᴵᵈ?EN??-x x⌝ [   ]
flatter side
1 a-lid
rest of side blank

Critical Apparatus

rounder side line 1: A tag hole goes through the top right corner.
line 3: The year number is written raised and small.

Translation
1 Night of the 16th, last part of the night.
2 Ṭebētu
3 Year 19 of Seleucus the king
4 Bēlšunu son of
5 Bēl-...(?) ...
6 was born.

Text 30 BM 33563

TEXT 31 (BM 34693 = SP II 180 (L* 1465)

S.E. 98 = -213

birth note, only one side inscribed

Transcription

1 MU.1,38.KAM KIN
2 LÚ a-lid MU.1.ME.⌈20+x.KAM⌉ U₄ 10+[ ]
3 1,38

Translation

1 Year 98 (S.E.), Ulūlu
2 the native was born. Year 120+ day 10+[...]
3 98

TEXT 31 BM 34693

TEXT 32 BM 34567

TEXT 32(BM 34567 = SP. II 39 [**1469])

S.E. 197 IV(?).9 = -114 July 3.
S.E. 194 XI.10 = -116 Jan. 30.
S.E. 158 IX.27= -153 Dec. 27.
Previous publication: A. Sachs, *JCS* 6, p.65.
photo: *JCS* 6, pl.IV.

Transcription

obv.
1 MU.1.ME.1,37.KAM
2 ITI.ŠU(?) U$_4$.9.KAM
3 pa-na-at KUR šamáš LÚ.TUR a-lid
4 MU.1.ME.1,34.KAM
5 ZÍZ GE$_6$10 30 DANNA
6 GE$_6$ ana ZALÁG LÚ.TUR a-lid
rev.
1 MU.1.ME.58.KAM
2 ITI.GAN GE$_6$ 27 ina MURUB$_4$-tim
3 LÚ.TUR a-lid

Critical Apparatus

2 Sachs suggests either ŠU month IV, or DU$_6$ month VII.

Translation

1 Year 197 (S.E.),
2 Du'ūzu(?) (or Tašrītu), the 9th,
3 before sunrise, the child was born.
4 Year 194 (S.E.),
5 Šabaṭu, night of the 10th, one-half *bēru* (= 1 hour)
6 remaining until sunrise, the child was born.
rev.
1 Year 158 (S.E.),
2 Kislīmu, night of the 27th, in the middle watch,
3 the child was born.

Abbreviations

ABCD: see Rochberg-Halton, ABCD.
ACT: see Neugebauer, ACT.
AfK: *Archiv für Keilschriftforschung.*
AfO: *Archiv für Orientforschung.*
AnOr: *Analecta Orientalia.*
AOAT: *Alter Orient und Altes Testament.*
Bagh. Mitt.: *Baghdader Mitteilungen.*
BPO: Babylonian Planetary Omens.
BRM: *Babylonian Records in the Library of J. Pierpont Morgan.*
CAD: *The Assyrian Dictionary of the University of Chicago.*
CRRAI: Compte rendu de la ... rencontre assyriologique internationale.
CT: *Cuneiform Texts from Babylonian Tablets in the British Museum.*
Gudea Cylinder: see Falkenstein.
HAMA: see Neugebauer, HAMA.
JAOS: *Journal of the American Oriental Society.*
JCS: *Journal of Cuneiform Studies.*
JHA: *Journal of the History of Astronomy.*
JNES: *Journal of Near Eastern Studies.*
MSL: *Materialien zum sumerischen Lexikon.*
OIP: Oriental Institute Publications.
OLZ: *Orientalische Literaturzeitung.*
RA: *Revue d'assyriologie et d'archéologie orientale.*
SBH: G.A. Reisner, *Sumerisch-babylonische Hymnen nach Thontafeln griechischer Zeit.*
SSB: see Kugler, SSB and SSB Erg.
SSB 3.Erg.: see Schaumberger.
TAPS: Transactions of the American Philosophical Society.
TCL: Textes Cunéiformes. Musée du Louvre.
YOS: *Yale Oriental Series.*
ZA: *Zeitschrift für Assyriologie.*

Bibliography

A: lexical series á A = *nâqu*, pub. Civil, MSL 14.

Aaboe, A. [1980]: "Observation and Theory in Babylonian Astronomy," *Centaurus* 24 (1980), pp.14-35.

—, Britton, J.P., Henderson, J.A., Neugebauer,O., and Sachs, A.J. [1991]: "Saros Cycle Dates and Related Babylonian Astronomical Texts TAPS 81/6 (1991).

— and Henderson, J.A. [1975]: "The Babylonian Theory of Lunar Latitude and Eclipses According to System A," *Archives internationales d'histoire des sciences* 15 (1975) 181-222.

— and Sachs, A.J. [1969]: "Two Lunar Texts of the Achaemenid Period from Babylon," *Centaurus* 14 (1969) 1-22.

ACh: C. Virolleaud, *L'Astrologie chaldéenne* (Paris: Paul Geuthner, 1909-1911)

Bakir, Cairo Cal.: Abd el-Mohsen Bakir, *The Cairo Calendar No.86637*. (Cairo: Antiquities Department of Egypt, 1966).

Beaulieu, P.-A. [1989]: "Textes administratifs inédits d'époque hellénistique provenant des archives du *Bīt Rēš*," RA 83 (1989) 53-87.

Bouché-Leclercq, A., *L'Astrologie grecque* (Paris: Leroux, 1899, reprinted Scientia Verlag Aalen, 1979).

Britton, J.P. [1989]: "An Early Function for Eclipse Magnitudes in Babylonian Astronomy," *Centaurus* 32 (1989) 1-52.

Cumont,F. [1935]: "Les nom des planetes et l'astroloatrie chez les Grecs," *L'Antiquité Classique* 4 (1935) 5-43.

Dandamaev, M.A., *Slavery in Babylonia: From Nabopolassar to Alexander the Great (626-331 B C)*, transl. by Victoria A. Powell, (De Kalb, Ill.: Northern Illinois University Press, rev. ed. 1984).

Debevoise, N.C., *A Political History of Parthia* (Chicago and London: University of Chicago Press, 1938).

Dorotheus of Sidon, *Carmen Astrologicum* ed. D. Pingree (Leipzig: Teubner, 1976).

Durand, J.-M., TBER: *Textes babyloniens d'époque récente* (Recherche sur les civilisations, Cahier n°6, Paris, 1981)

Epping, J. [1889]: "Aus einem Briefe desselben an J.N. Strassmaier" ZA 4 (1889) 168-171.

Falkenstein, A., *Die Inschriften Gudeas von Lagash: Einleitung* (AnOr 30, Rome: Pontificium Institutum Biblicum, 1966).

Frye, Richard N., *The History of Ancient Iran* (Munich: C.H.Beck, 1984).

Goetze, A., *Old Babylonian Omen Texts* (YOS 10, New Haven and London: Yale University Press, 1947).

Goldstein, B.R. [1985]: review of G. Toomer, *Ptolemy's Almagest, Isis* 76 (1985), 117-118.

Goldstein, B.R. and Bowen, A.C. [1989]: "On Early Hellenistic Astronomy: Timocharis and the First Callippic Calendar," *Centaurus* 32 (1989) 272-293.

Hephaestion of Thebes, *Apotelesmatica*, ed. D. Pingree (Leipzig: Teubner, 1973)

Hg.: lexical series HAR.gud = *imrû* = *ballu*, pub. MSL 5-11.

Hunger Kolophone: H. Hunger, *Babylonische und assyrische Kolophone* (=AOAT 2, Kevelaer und Neukirchen-Vluyn, 1968).

Hunger Uruk: H. Hunger, *Spätbabylonische Texte aus Uruk 1* (Ausgrabungen der deutschen Forschungsgemeinschaft in Uruk-Warka Band 9, Berlin: Gebr. Mann, 19).

Hunger,H. and Dvorak, R., *Ephemeriden von Sonne, Mond und hellen Planeten von -1000 bis -601* (Verlag der Österreichischen Akademie der Wissenschaften, Vienna, 1981)

Hunger, H. and Pingree, D., *MUL.APIN: An Astronomical Compendium in Cuneiform* (AfO Beiheft 24, Vienna, 1989).

King STC: King, L.W., *The Seven Tablets of Creation* 2 vols. (London: Luzac, 1902).

Klíma, J. [1964], "Beiträge zur Struktur der neubabylonischen Gesellschaft," CRRAI 11(Leiden, 1964) 11-21.

Koch-Westenholz, U., *Mesopotamian Astrology: An Introduction to Babylonian and Assyrian Celestial Divination* (Copenhagen: Carsten Niebuhr Institute Publications 19, 1995).

Kraus Texte: F.R. Kraus, *Texte zur babylonischen Physiognomatik* (AfO Beiheft 3, Berlin, 1939).

Kugler SSB: F.X. Kugler, *Sternkunde und Sterndienst in Babel: Assyriologicshe, Astronomische und Astralmythologische Untersuchungen* 2 vols. and, *Ergänzungen zum ersten und zweiten Buch* (Münster: Aschendorff, 1907, 1909-1924).

Labat Calendrier: René Labat, *Un calendrier babylonien des travaux des signes et des mois (séries iqqur ipuš)* (Paris: Bibliothèque de l'École des Hautes Études IVᵉ sect., fasc. 321, 1965).

Langdon, S, *Babylonian Menologies and the Semitic Calendars* (London: Oxford University Press, 1935).

Landsberger, B. [1923], "Ein astralmythologischer Kommentar aus der Spätzeit babylonischer Gelehrsamkeit," AfK 1 (1923) 69-82.

LBAT: see Pinches-Sachs, LBAT.

Livingstone, A., *Mystical and Mythological Explanatory Works of Assyrian and Babylonian Scholars* (Oxford: The Clarendon Press, 1986).

Malku: synonym list *malku* = *šarru* (Malku I pub. A.D. Kilmer, JAOS 83 421ff.)

Manilius, *Astronomica*, ed. and transl. G.P. Goold (Cambridge, Mass. and London: Loeb Classical Library, 1977).

Mayer, W., [1978]: "Seleukidische Rituale aus Warka mit Emesal-Gebeten," OrNS 47 (1978) 431-458.

McEwan, J.P., *Priest and Temple in Hellenistic Babylonia* (Freiburger altorientalische Studien Band 4, Wiesbaden, 1981).

Meissner, B., [1925]: "Über Genethlialogie bei den Babyloniern," *Klio* 19 (1925) 432-434.

Neugebauer, O., [1947]: "A Table of Solstices from Uruk," JCS 1 (1947) 143-148.

— , [1948]: "Solstices and Equinoxes in Babylonian Astronomy," JCS 2 (1948) 209-222.

— , [1963]: "Demotic Horoscopes," JAOS 63 (1943) 116-126.

Neugebauer, ACT: O. Neugebauer, *Astronomical Cuneiform Texts* 3 vols. (London: Lund Humphries, 1955).

Neugebauer, HAMA: O. Neugebauer, *A History of Ancient Mathematical Astronomy*. 3 vols. (Berlin, Heidelberg, and New York: Springer, 1975).

— and Sachs, A.J., [1967]: "Some Atypical Astronomical Cuneiform Texts. I," JCS 21 (1967) 183-218.

— and Sachs, A.J., [1969]: "Some Atypical Astronomical Cuneiform Texts. II," JCS 22 (1969) 92-113.

— and van Hoesen, H.B., *Greek Horoscopes* (Memoirs of the American Philosophical Society 48, Philadelphia: American Philosophical Society, 1959).

North, J.D., *Horoscopes and History* (Warburg Institute Surveys and Texts XIII, London: The Warburg Institute, University of London, 1986).

Oelsner, J., *Materialien zur babylonischen Gesellschaft und Kultur in hellenistischer Zeit* (Budapest: Assyriologia VII, 1986).

Offner, G., [1950]: "À propos de la sauvegarde des tablettes en Assyro-Babylonie, " RA 44 (1950) 135-143.

Oppenheim, A.L., *Ancient Mesopotamia: Portrait of a Dead Civilization*, rev.ed. by Erica Reiner (Chicago and London: University of Chicago Press, 1977).

— , "Man and Nature in Mesopotamian Civilization," *Dictionary of Scientific Biography* Vol.15 (1977).

Oppolzer Canon: Th.v. Oppolzer, *Canon der Finsternisse*. (Math.-Naturwiss. Cl. d. ... Akad. d. Wiss. Denkschriften 52, Vienna, 1887).

Pallis, S.A., "The History of Babylon 538-93 B.C.," in F. Hvidberg ed.,

Studia Orientalia Ioanni Pedersen Septuagenario (Haunia: Munksgaard, 1953) 275-294.

Parker, R.A. and Dubberstein, W.H., *Babylonian Chronology 626 B.C.- A.D. 75* (Providence, R.I.: Brown University Press, 1956, 1971 4th ed.).

PD: see Parker-Dubberstein, *Babylonian Chronology*.

Pinches, T.G. and Strassmaier, J.N. and Sachs, A.J., *Late Babylonian Astronomical and Related Texts* (Providence, R.I.:Brown University Press, 1955).

Pingree, D., "Petosiris," *Dictionary of Scientific Biography* Vol. 10 (New York: Scribners, 1974) 547-549.

—, "Astrology," in P.P. Wiener, ed., *Dictionary for the History of Ideas* Vol. I (New York: Scribner, 1968, 1973) 118-126.

—, *The Yavanajātaka of Sphujidhvaja* 2 vols. (Harvard Oriental Series 48, Cambridge, Mass. and London: Harvard University Press, 1978).

Ptolemy, *Tetrabiblos*, ed. and transl. by F.E. Robbins (Cambridge, Mass. and London: Loeb Classical Library, 1940).

Powell, M., "Masse und Gewichte," in *Reallexikon der Assyriologie und Vorderasiatischen Archäologie* (Berlin: Walter de Gruyter, 1987-1990)457-517.

Reiner, E. and Pingree, D., *BPO 2: Enūma Anu Enlil Tablets 50-51* (Bibliotheca Mesopotamica 2, Malibu: Undena Publications, 1981).

— and Pingree, D., [1977]: "A Neo-Babylonian Report on Seasonal Hours," AfO 25 (1977) 50-55.

Riemschneider, K., *Babylonische Geburtsomina in hethitischer Übersetzung* (Studien zu den Boghazköy Texten 9, Wiesbaden, 1970).

Riess, E., *Nechepsonis et Petosiridis fragmenta magica* (Philologus Suppl. 6, 1892).

Rochberg-Halton, F., [1987]: "Mixed Traditions in Late Babylonian Astrology," ZA 77 (1987) 207-228.

—, [1987]: "Elements of the Babylonian Contribution to Hellenistic Astrology," JAOS 108 (1987) 51-62.

Rochberg-Halton, ABCD: F. Rochberg-Halton, *Aspects of Babylonian Celestial Divination: The Lunar Eclipse Tablets of Enūma Anu Enlil* (AfO Beiheft 22, Vienna,1988).

—, "Benefics and Malefics in Babylonian Astrology," in Leichty et al., eds., *A Scientific Humanist: Studies in Memory of Abraham Sachs* (Occasional Publications of the Samuel Noah Kramer Fund 9, Philadelphia, Pa, 1988) 323-328.

—, [1989a]: "Seasonal Hours in Babylonian Astronomy," *Centaurus* 32 (1989) 146-170.

—, [1989b]: "Babylonian Horoscopes and Their Sources," OrNS 58 (1989) 102-123.

Roth, M.T., "A Case of Contested Status, " in *DUMU-E₂-DUB-BA-A: Studies in Honor of Åke Sjöberg* (Occasional Publications of the Samuel Noah Kramer Fund 11, Philadelphia, 1989).

—, [1988]: "*ina amat* DN₁ *u* DN₂ *lišlim*," *Journal of Semitic Studies* 33 (1988) 1-9.

Sachs, A.J., [1967]: "Naissance de'astrologie horoscopique en Babylonie," *Archaeologia* 15 (1967) 13-19.

—, [1948]: "A Classification of the Babylonian Astronomical Tablets of the Seleucid Period," JCS 2 (1948) 271-290.

—, [1952]: "Babylonian Horoscopes," JCS 6 (1952) 49-75, pls. III-IV.

—, "The Last Dateable Cuneiform Texts," in *Kramer Anniversary Volume* (AOAT 25, Neukirchen, 1976) 379-398.

—, [1977]: "Achaemenid Royal Names in Babylonian Astronomical Texts," *American Journal of Ancient History* 2 (1977) 129-147.

Sachs-Hunger *Diaries*: Sachs, A.J. and Hunger, H., *Astronomical Diaries and Related Texts from Babylonia* 3 vols. (Vienna: Österreichische Akademie der Wissenschaften, 1988-1996).

— and Walker, C.B.F., [1984]: "Kepler's View of the Star of Bethlehem and the Babylonian Almanac for 7/6 B.C.," *Iraq* 46 (1984) 4-55.

Schaumberger, J., *Sternkunde und Sterndienst in Babel, 3. Ergänzungsheft zum ersten und zweiten Buch* (Münster: Aschendorff, 1935).

—, "Der Jüngste Datierbare Keilschrifttext (Sp II 142, eine Planetentafel aus der Zeit um Christi Geburt)," AnOr 12 (Rome: Pontificium Institutum Biblicum, 1935) 279-287.

Slotsky, A., "The Uruk Solstice Scheme Revisited," in H. Galter ed., *Die Rolle der Astronomie in den Kulturen Mesopotamiens* (Beiträge zum 3. Grazer Morgenländischen Symposion, 1993) 359-366.

Stephenson, F.R. and Fatoohi, L.J., [1993]: "Lunar Eclipse Times Recorded in Babylonian History," JHA 24 (1993) 255-267.

— and Fatoohi, L.J., [1994]: "The Babylonian Unit of Time," JHA 25 (1994) 99-10.

Stieglitz, R.R., "The Chaldeo-Babylonian Planet Names in Hesychius," Y.L. Arbeitman ed., *Fucus: A Semitic/Afrasian Gathering in Remembrance of Albert Ehrman* (*Current Issues in Linguistic Theory* 58 [1988]) 443-447.

Strassmaier, J.N., [1888]: "Arsaciden-Inschriften," ZA 3 (1888) 129-158.

TBER: see Durand, J.-M., TBER

Thompson, R.C., *A Catalogue of the Late Babylonian Tablets in the Bodleian Library Oxford* (London: Luzac, 1927).

Thureau-Dangin, F., *Tablettes d'Uruk* (TCL 6, Paris: Paul Geuthner, 1922).

Tuckerman, B., *Planetary, Lunar and Solar Positions: 601 BC to AD 1*
       (Memoirs of the American Philosophical Society 56, Philadelphia,
       1962).

Ungnad, A., [1941-44]: "Besprechungskunst und Astrologie in Babylonien,"
       AfO 14 (1941-44) 251-282.

Vettius Valens, *Anthologiae*, ed. D. Pingree (Leipzig: Teubner, 1986).

Weidner, E. [1913]: "Beiträge zur Erklärung der astronomischen
       Keilschrifttexte," OLZ (1913) 208-210.

—, [1919]: "Babylonische Hypsomatabilder," OLZ (1919) 10-16.

—, *Gestirn-Darstellungen aus babylonischen Tontafeln* (Österreichische
       Akademie der Wissenschaften, Philos.-histor. Kl. S.B. 254, 2 [1967]).

General Glossary

A

A "Leo": passim
A (*aplu*) "son" 2:2; 4 r.5; 15:1; 30:4
Á.TUK (*nēmelu*) "profit" 5 r.10
AB (*Ṭebētu*) "Month X"
    ITI.AB: 1:1; 8 r.1; 9:1
    AB: 1:4, r. 4; 23:2
    ITI.AB.KAM 30:2
ABSIN "Virgo": passim
AD (*abu*) "father" 10 r.3; 11 r.4
ád (for *adriš*) "darkly"
    ád È-*a* "(moon) rose darkly (meaning, eclipsed)" 27 r.7
ahu see ŠEŠ
al (for *alla*) "beyond, exceeding"
    al šal HAB-*rat* "(lunar eclipse) exceeding one-third disk" 27 r.6
akalu "bread, food" 5 r.4
alādu "to give birth, (stative) to be born"
    LÚ *a-lid* "the native was born" 13:4, r. 7; 14:5; 31:2
    LÚ.TUR *a-lid* "the native (literally: child) was born" : passim
    PN *a-lid* 2:2; 4 r. 5; 9:2; 10:2; 11:2; 12:3
    ina bīt niṣirti ša zodiacal sign$_x$ *a-lid* 6:4'; 8 r. 3; 18 r.4
alāku see GIN
alla "beyond, exceeding" see also *al*
    al-la 2-⌈*ta*⌉ [ŠU^{II}(?)] HAB-*rat* "exceeding two-thirds of the disk" 21 r.2
ALLA "Cancer": passim
amāru see IGI
ammatu see KÙŠ
AN (*Ṣalbatānu*) "Mars": passim
ana (DIŠ) "to"
    ana ME.E 1 r. 4
     ME *ana* ŠÚ 6 r. 3
     TA MURUB$_4$ *ana* (var. *a-na*) NIM 10:4, 5; 11:4, 5
    ana MURUB$_4$ 16:9, r.10
    ana NIM DIB 7 r.3; 13:4; 14:4
    GE$_6$ *ana* ZALÁG 32:6
AN.KU$_{10}$ (*attalû*) "eclipse": passim
APIN (*Araḫsamna*) "Month VIII"
aplu see A
ár (*arki*) "after, behind" 1:3; 6 r.2; 14:3
arāku see GÍD

155

arhu see ITI
arhussu "each month" 10 r.5; 11 r.6
arkû see DIRI
aṣû see È
ašarēdu see SAG.KAL
aššatu see DAM
atāru see DIRI
attalû see AN.KU₁₀

B

BABBAR also MÚL.BABBAR "Jupiter": passim
banû "to be propitious" 2 r.1
BAR also ITI.BAR (*Nisannu*) "Month I": passim, see also BARA₂
BAR (*mišlu*) "one-half"
    AN.[KU₁₀ *šamáš*] *ina* HUN BAR DIB "a [solar ecl]ipse in Aries; one-half
    (month?) passed by" 14 r. 6; cf. 20 r.4, and 24 r. 1. Meaning is uncertain.
BARA₂ (*Nisannu*) "Month I" 2:1
BE (*šumma*) "if" 10:5; 11:5; 16 r.9
bēru see DANNA
birītu "between" 5 r. 11
birû "hunger" 5 r. 4
bītu see É
bubbulu see U₄.NÁ.ÀM

D

DAM (*aššatu*) "wife" 5 r. 8
DANNA (*bēru*) "an astronomical unit (30°) 6 r.3; 32:5
dannu see KALAG
DELE (*ēdu*) "single"
    DELE *šá* IGI ABSIN "The Single star in front of the Furrow" 6 r. 2
⁽ᵈ⁾*delebat* "Venus" : passim
DI (*šalāmu*) "to be well" 10:7
DIB (*etēqu*) "to pass by" passim
    (*ṣabātu*) "to take" 9:[5]
DIRI (*arkû*) in the intercalary Month XII ŠE DIRI: 1:6, r.5
    (*atāru*) 21 r.3; 22 r? 16'; 27 r.6
    (*erpetu*) "cloud" 1:5
DU₆ (*Tašrītu*) "Month VII" 5:11; 14:2; 16:[1]; 19:8; 17:1
DUGUD (*kabātu*) "to become important" 10 r.3
dumqu see SIG₅
DUMU (*māru*) "son" 2:2; 9:6; 10:10; 11:[11]
DUMU.SAL (*mārtu*) 10:10; 11:11; 17 r.3

E

É (*bītu*) "house" 10 r.3; 11 r. 4; 5:10, 11

in *bīt niṣirti* "secret house" 3:4'; 6:4'; 8 r.2; 13 r.6; 15 r.3; 18 r.3
È (*aṣû*) "to rise"
    ád È-*a* 27 r.7
ēdu see DELE
ēma "wherever" 10:9
erpetu see DIRI
etēqu see DIB

G

gamartum see TIL
GAN (*Kislīmu*) "Month IX" 1 r.4; 7 r.1; 14 r.2; 17:3; 23:8; 24:2; 32:8
GAR (*šakānu*) "to set, establish"
    (the moon) *pānišu ana* MURUB$_4$ GAR.MEŠ "(the moon) set its face toward
       the node" 16:9, r.10; 10:4, 5; 11:6
      n SI GAR-*an* "(the eclipse) made n fingers" 20 r.5; 26 r.5
      (with designations of the amount of the disk eclipsed) 21 r.3; 22 r. 16'; 27
        r.7
      TIL-*tim* GAR-*an* "to establish (eclipse) totality" 4 r.4; 14 r.4
GE$_6$ (*mūšu*) "night": passim
      GE$_6$ *ana* ZALÁG "(so many units of) night until sunrise" 32:6
GENNA (*Kajamānu*) "Saturn": passim
GI (*šalāmu*) "to prosper" 10:7
GÍD, GÍD.DA (*arāku*) "to be long"
       U$_4$. MEŠ GÍD.DA(.MEŠ) "long days (=life)" 5 r.7; 9:4; 10:8
GIGIR (*narkabtu*) "chariot" see ŠUR GIGIR
GIN (*alāku*) "to go" 10:9
GÍR.TAB (*Zuqaqīpu*) "Scorpius": passim
GU "Aquarius": passim
GU$_4$ (*Ajaru*) "Month II": passim
GU$_4$.AN "Taurus" 2:5
GU$_4$.UD (*Šiḫṭu*) "Mercury": passim
    written GU$_4$ 5:7; 16:6, r.6
GUB (*uzuzzu*) "to stand, to be present"
    (planet) *ina* 3 RÍN GUB-*zu* 11:7; 16 r.7,8
    šamáš GUB (*izziz(a)*) "solstice": passim; written ^{d}UTU GUB 7 r.4

H

HAB-*rat* "disk" 21 r.3; 22 r? 16'; 27 r.6
harrānu see KASKAL
HUN abbreviated writing for ^{LÚ}HUN.GÁ (*Agru*) "Aries": passim

I

IGI (*amāru*) "to see"
    Á.TUK IGI-*ir* 5 r.10; cf. 16:10.

(*amāru, nanmuru*) "to be seen, to be visible"
  NU IGI "not visible" 2:[6]; 13:8; 14:[8]; 15:7; 21:6; NU IGI.MEŠ 19:6;
   20:9; 21 r.5; 24:8, r.3; 27:7, r.3
  (*pānu*) "front"
    ina IGI-*ka* "before you, in your presence" 2 r.1;
    ina IGI (star name) "in front of star such-and-such" 1:6; 4:3; 15:3; 18:3
    in names of stars: DELE *ša* IGI ABSIN 6 r.2; MUL IGI *ša* SAG HUN
     7:2
  (*tāmartu*) "appearance; first visibility" 1:3, r.3, r.4; 16 r.5; 24:6; 26:[8]
IGI^{II} (*īnā*) "eyes" 5 r.2
ina "in" : passim
inūšu "at that time" 2:3; 4:4; 7 r. up.edge 1
ištu see TA
ITI (*arhu*) "month": passim
  ITI.BI (*arhu šû*) "that month": passim
  ITI-*us-su* see *arhussu*

K

kabātu see DUGUD
Kajamānu see GENNA
kakkabu see MUL, also MÚL
KALAG (*dannu*) "dense" 1:5
KASKAL (*harrānu*) "road" 5 r.11
kašādu see KUR
kī "when" 21 r.5; 22 r? 7'; 27 r.3
KI (*itti*) "with": passim
  (*qaqqaru*) "place" KI GU$_4$.UD "the place of Mercury" 10 r.1
KIN (*Ulūlu*) ITI.KIN "Month VI": passim
KUN (*zibbātu*) "tails, Pisces" 1 r.2; written KUN.MEŠ 2:4; see also ZIB.ME
KUR (*napāhu*) "to rise"
  "last (lunar) visibility (= rising of the moon just before sunrise) of
   the month" : passim
  "east" from KUR (*nipih*) *Šamši* "the rising of the sun": (planet) U$_4$.BI *ina*
   KUR "that day (the planet) ... in the east" 16 r.5;
  itti KUR *šamáš* "with sunrise" 29:2; 32:3
KUR (*kašādu*) "to reach" 16 r.6
KÙŠ (*ammatu*) "cubit: 2°": passim

L

LÁ (*maţû*) "to decrease, be lacking" 5 r.2
labāru see SUMUN
LAL (*šaqû*) "to reach positive latitude" 16 r. 10
LÁL (*šitqultu*)"equinox" 4 r.2; 7:3; 18 r.2; 19:8; 21:7
lapani "before" la-pa-ni AN.KU$_{10}$ s[in] "before the lu[nar] eclipse" 3:5'
leû "to overpower someone" 5 r.9

LU for LÚ.HUN "Aries" 28 r? 3; 5:3
LÚ abbreviated writing of LÚ.TUR (*šerru*) "native" 13:4; 14:5; 31:2
LÚ.TUR (*šerru*) "child, native": passim
LUGAL (*šarru*) "king" : passim; LUGAL.MEŠ 4:1; 15:1

M

magāru see ŠE.GA
mamma "someone" 9:5
mārtu see DUMU
māru see DUMU.SAL
MAŠ abbreviation for MAŠ.MAŠ "Gemini" 16 r.5
MAŠ.MAŠ "Gemini" : passim
MÁŠ "Capricorn" : passim
mašrû see NÍG.TUK
maṭû see LÁ
ME (*ūmu*) "daylight"
     ME *ana* ŠÚ "(so many units of) daylight until sunset" 6 r.3
ME.E "opposition" (also ME.A and E.ME)
    ana ME.E 1 r.4
mišlu "middle" see also BAR
    [*m*]*i-šil* GE$_6$ middle of night 24:3
MU (*šattu*) "year": passim
muhhu "concerning" 5 r.11; see also UGU
MUL, MÚL (*kakkabu*) "star" 7:2; 14:3
   abbreviation for MÚL.MÚL "Taurus" 16:3, r.8
MÚL.MÚL "Taurus" 4 r.4'
MURUB$_4$ (*qablītu*) "nodal zone" 10:4,5; 11:4,5; 16:9, r.10
     (*qablītu*) "middle (watch)" 32:8
mūšu see GE$_6$

N

NA or *na* (for *nanmurtu*) "moonset after sunrise" 7 r.5; 8:9; 13 r.1; 14 r.1; 15
r.1; 18:8; 19:7; 20:3; 21:7; 22 r. 13'; 23:7; 25:8 27 r.1
namāru see ZALÁG
napāhu see KUR
narkabtu see GIGIR
nasāhu see ZI
naṣāru see PAP
nēmelu see Á.TUK
nenmudu see UŠ
nēšu see UR.A
NÍG.ŠID (*nikkassu*) "property" 5 r.2, 5, 6, 11
NÍG.TUK (*mašrû*) "wealth" 10:7; 11:8
nikkassu see NÍG.ŠID

NIM (*šaqû*) "to be high" NIM TUR "(it was) high (and) faint" 1 r.3
    (*šûqu*) "(maximum) positive latitude" *ana* NIM "toward the top" 10:4, 5;
    11:4, 5
    as abbreviated writing for GIŠ.NIM (*šītān*) "east" 1:3, 5, 6; 6:3'; 7 r. 3, up.
    edge 2; 13:4; 14:4; 24:6; 26:7; 28 r.(?)2
nišū see UKÙ.MEŠ
NU (*ul*) "negation"
NUN (*rubû*) "prince" 9:5

P

PA "Sagittarius": passim
pānu "before" 5 r.8; 32:3
    "face" 10:4, 5; 11:4, 6; 16:9, r. 10
PAP (*naṣāru*) "to watch, observe" 21 r.5; 22 r? 7'; 27 r.3

Q

qablītu see MURUB₄
qarnu see SI
qarradu "hero" 10 r. 1; 11 r. 1
qatû see TIL
qātu "hand" 9:5
qītu see TIL

R

ra'āmu "love" 5:17
rabbûtu "greatness" 10:6
rabû see ŠÚ
rašû see TUK
rēšu see SAG
RÍN "Libra": passim
rubû see NUN

S

SAG (*rēšu*) "beginning"
    SAG GE₆ "beginning of night": passim
    SAG zodiacal sign name "beginning of sign ..." 7:2; 5:5; 9:5; 14:3;
      21:4, r.2
SAG.KAL (*ašarēdu*) "first in rank" 10 [r.2]
SAL (*sinništu*) "woman" 5 r.10
SI (*qarnu*) "horn" 2:3
    (*ubānu*) "finger" 20 r.5; 26 r. 5
SIG (*šaplu*) "below" 7:2, r.2; 13:3; 14:3
    (*šuplu*) "(minimum) negative latitude" 16:9
SIG (*Simānu*) "Month III" 16 r. 1; 26 r.1; ITI.SIG 22:6'
SIG₅ (*damqu*) "propitious" 16:10; r.9;

(*dumqu*) "prosperity; fortune" 10:6; 11:6
SILIM (*šalāmu*) "to be at peace" 10:7
simānu "hour" (usually written *si-man*) 6 r.4; 8:4(?); 13:5; 14:5; 15:5; 18:5; 19:3;
      20:5; 21:3, 4; 22 r? 2', 10'; 23:3; 24:4; 25:2; 26:3; 27:2, 3
ᵈSin "moon" (written 30): passim
sinništu see SAL
SUMUN (*labāru*) "to last a long time" 10:7; 11:8

Ṣ

Ṣalbatānu "Mars" see AN
Ṣehēru see TUR
Ṣehru see TUR
Ṣētu see UD.DA
Ṣītān see NIM

Š

ša "of, which": passim
šal "one-third" 27 r.6
šalāmu see DI
ᵈ*Šamaš* "sun" (written 20): passim
šaplâtu "below" 2:3
šaqû see LAL; also NIM
šarru see LUGAL
šattu see MU
ŠE (*Addaru*) "Month XII" : passim
ŠE.GA (*magāru*) "to find favor" 10:9
šerru see LÚ.TUR; also LÚ
ŠEŠ (*ahu*) "brother" 10 r.3
Šihṭu see GU₄.UD "Mars"
šitqultu see LÁL "equinox"
šû "he, it"
      šú-ú "it is" 3:3'
ŠU (*Du'ūzu*) "Month IV": passim
ŠÚ (*rabû*) "to set"
      ša ŠÚ-*ú* "(the planet) which had set" 2:6; 8:7; 13:8; 15:7; 19:6; 20:8; 21:6;
      22 r.? 12'; 24:[8]; 25:5; 27:7
      ŠÚ *Šamaš* "sunset" 6 r.3; 27 r.5
   in the meaning "last visibility" or "disappearance" 1:5, 6, r.2; 4:6, 7; 6:3'; 7
   upper edge 2;
šumma see BE
šuplu see SIG
šūqu see NIM
šūtu see ULÙ

T

TA (*ištu*) "from": passim

TIL (*gamartu*) "totality" 4 r.4; 14 r.4; 22 r.? 8'; 23 edge
    (*qītu*) "end" 5:9; 15:5; 20 r.5; 27:3,4; r.4

TUK (*rašû*) "to have" 5 r.5, 6, 10; 9:6; 10:10

TUR (*ṣehēru*) "to be young" *ina* TUR-*šú* "in his youth" 5 r.5
    (*ṣehru*) "small, faint" 1 r.3; 29:5

U

U₄ (*ūmu*) "day": passim

U₄.NÁ.ÀM (*bubbulu*) "last visibility of the moon" 2:8

UD.DA (*ṣētu*) "first visibility" 6:3'

UGU (*muhhu*) "(in prepositional use) over" 10 r.3

UKÙ.MEŠ (*nišū*) "people" 5 r.8

ul see NU

ULÙ (*šūtu*) "south" 4:3; 15:3

ūmu see ME; see also U₄

UR.A (*nēšu*) "Leo" 4 r.1

USÁN (*barārītu*) "morning watch" 15:4; 19:2

UŠ (*nenmudu*) "to be at a stationary point" 1 r.1, 4; 10:6

ᵈUTU see *Šamaš* 3:3'; 4 r.1; 7 r.4; 8:5; 13:6

uzuzzu see GUB

Z

ZALÁG (*namāru*) "last part of night": passim

ZI (*nasāhu*) "progress (in longitude)" 16 r.9

zibbātu see KUN; also ZIB.ME

ZIB.ME (*zibbātu*) "tails, the zodiacal sign Pisces" 7:4; 20 r.3; 21:5, r.2; 27 r.8

ZÍZ (*Šabaṭu*) "Month XI": passim

INDEX TO TEXTS CITED